MAY, 1994

SALLY WILLIAMS,

HOPE YOU ENJOY THE

BOOK.

P. Rose

PAW PAW LAKE, MICHIGAN

A 100 YEAR RESORT HISTORY

(1890's - 1990's)

by R. L. Rasmussen

Southwestern Michigan Publications
Coloma, Michigan

Paw Paw Lake, Michigan A 100 Year Resort History (1890's -1990's)

First Edition 1994   © Copyright 1994 by Roderick L. Rasmussen

DUST JACKET AND COVER: Robin Maxon of Maxon Graphics and Design

DRAWINGS: Sherry Holland

MAP DESIGNS: Steven Monsen and Brian Hartmann

PHOTOGRAPHER: Marv Causey

EDITORS: Trisha Dean and Deborah Fralick

PRINTING: R. W. Patterson Printing Co.

PUBLISHER: Southwestern Michigan Publications

TYPIST: Patricia Olson

Library of Congress Catalog Number: 94-65459

ISBN Hardcover 0-9640093-0-7   Softbound 0-9640093-1-5

Published by
Southwestern Michigan Publications
P.O. Box 916
Coloma, Michigan 49038

This book is dedicated to all the people who played a part in the lake's development and to those generations of people who have just enjoyed Paw Paw Lake.

A SPECIAL ACKNOWLEDGMENT

In the back of this book you will find a list of people and institutions who made this project a reality. On this page I wish to thank and acknowledge the communities that make up Paw Paw Lake.

The author Thomas Wolfe wrote a book titled <u>You Can't Go Home Again</u>. This is based on his own experience of returning to his hometown and being disillusioned by what he sees. I have had a much different experience than Thomas Wolfe. In fact I found you can go back home and find it a joy to write about its history.

Having left Paw Paw Lake after my childhood and just coming back to visit family and friends, I wasn't sure if I could reconnect or feel that I still belonged. But I quickly found those values of friendliness, openness, and trust are still there, and I felt at home again. For these values and sense of heritage, this book was able to be written.

Roderick L. Rasmussen

TABLE OF CONTENTS

MAPS

INTRODUCTION

Three questions need to be addressed for the reader of this book.

1. Where is Paw Paw Lake?

2. Why write a book about Paw Paw Lake now?

3. Who wants to read a book about Paw Paw Lake.

INTRODUCTION

1.   Where is Paw Paw Lake.

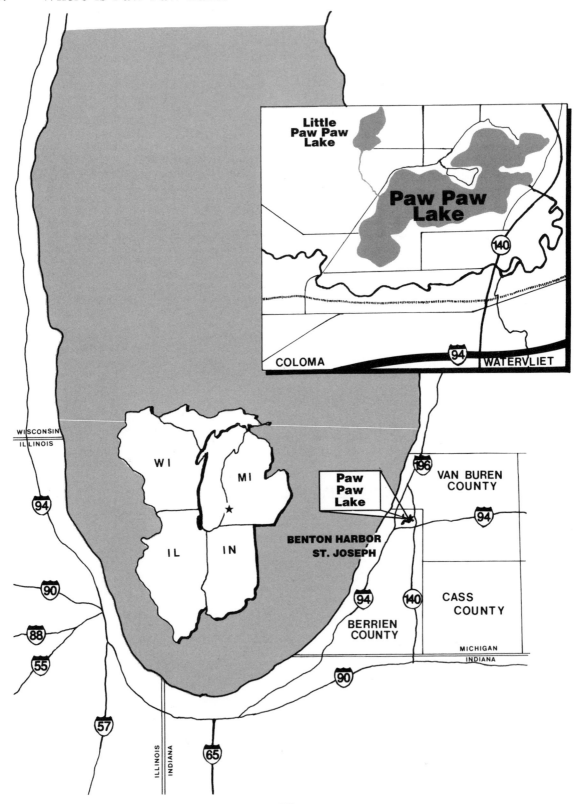

INTRODUCTION

2.   Why write a book about Paw Paw Lake now?

The answer to that question is that it is the perfect time. Paw Paw Lake's history will soon touch the third century of vacationers. During the 1990's the lake will be observing its 100th anniversary as a resort destination.

Starting in the 1890's the character of Paw Paw Lake changed forever. J. H. Jones built the first hotel in 1890. In 1893 the first group of Chicago vacationers stayed at Spenser's Farm. Dr. W. A. Baker built a train line to Paw Paw Lake in 1896. By 1899 the construction of Woodward's Pavilion had begun. This book uses that 10 year period of events to begin to tell the history of Paw Paw Lake these last 100 years.

3.   Who wants to read a book about Paw Paw Lake?

This book is directed toward three groups of readers. First, this book is for that group of readers who have had contact with Paw Paw Lake - for all those people who swam in it, sailed on it, built cottages around it, and even danced on it. During its peak years as a resort destination, over 50,000 people came to Paw Paw Lake each season. Hopefully, this book will evoke memories for some of those people and families who have enjoyed the lake for the last hundred years.

Second, that group of readers who are interested in southwestern Michigan history and regional American history. Paw Paw Lake is viewed from its geographical location in the country of Berrien, state of Michigan, section of the Great Lakes and region of the Midwest. Each one of these areas

INTRODUCTION

influenced and shaped the others. The towns of Coloma and Watervliet, Michigan, cities of Benton Harbor and St. Joseph, Michigan, and the metropolis of Chicago, Illinois, provided the sources for Paw Paw Lake's growth. These communities were inter-connected with each other and all had a relationship to Paw Paw Lake. The farmers and merchants, Chicago residents and town folks, businessmen and vacationers, all played their role in the lake's history.

Third, that group of readers who just enjoy American history. Starting in the 1890's America emerged on to the world scene as the most powerful and influential nation on earth. We as a country have came of age in the last 100 years. The 20th century has been the "American Experience." This nation's values and attitudes set the tone for Paw Paw Lake's development. The need and desire to grow, to build and expand as a way of life, is reflected time and again in Paw Paw Lake's history. This same process of development was also taking place at hundreds of other lakes across this country during the same time period. Paw Paw Lake's heritage is America's heritage.

Chapter 1

THE LAND

We as a people have been shaped by our land. The desire to obtain it, the work to change it, and the dreams to use it have given us part of our identity as a nation. In conquering the land we have come to believe that anything is possible. In this book you will see some of those forces played out in the people and events of the lands surrounding Paw Paw Lake.

The focus of this book is on the last 100 years, but we can trace this process back 200 years to 1794. In November of that year the Jay Treaty was signed between Great Britain and the United States of America. That document opened up and gave control of this Northwest Territory to a new nation and its people.

THE LAND   Chapter 1

Until the 1820's this part of Michigan, which was not yet a state, was almost untouched by white men. After taking the land or buying it from the Indians, the U.S. government sold much of the land to eastern speculators and timber companies. They in turn sold property often sight unseen to newly arriving immigrants from Europe. These settlers came with the intention of farming the land or taking its timber. During the Civil War from 1861 to 1865 much of this territory was going for $5 per acre for timberland and $10 per acre for cleared land. Property that had lake frontage was strictly incidental to any buyers of the land. This attitude toward land around Paw Paw Lake continued for another 25 years.

Starting in the 1890's, this perception and use of lake property started to change. To use a cliche, "Paw Paw Lake was at the right place at the right time." America's industrialization, lifestyles, and inventions were going to change the use of Paw Paw Lake's lands forever. With the 1890's the lake started experiencing a "ripple effect." During these years there was a steady stream of people coming from Chicago by boat to Benton Harbor and St. Joseph, Michigan, to take in the mineral baths, to escape the city heat, and to enjoy the beaches of Lake Michigan. It even became fashionable to come over for the day to St. Joseph by boat and get married at the St. Joseph Courthouse. Vacationers also started to "ripple" over to the surrounding countryside to have a rural experience. The refreshing waters of Paw Paw Lake started to be discovered by Chicago people. At the same time, local folks from the towns of Coloma, Watervliet and Hartford were "rippling" out to the lake to dine, camp, and fish. Both groups started realizing the potential the lake had to offer.

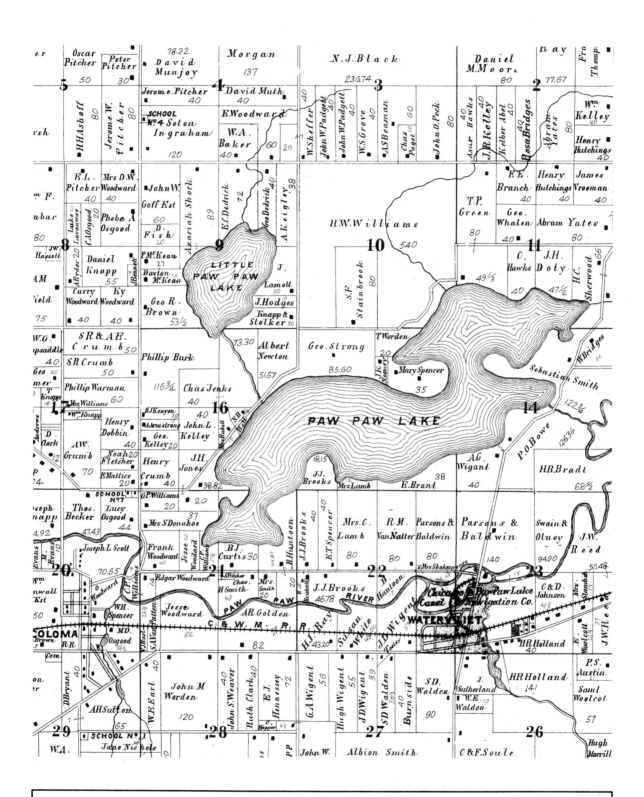

An 1887 Plat Map of Paw Paw Lake Area of Waltervliet Township.

THE LAND   Chapter 1

The golden era of Paw Paw Lake as a resort destination had begun. The farms and forests surrounding the lake were ready to take on a new way of life. The year 1890 saw the start of a new direction for Paw Paw Lake property. J.H. Jones, a farmer on the Coloma side of the lake, who owned 38 acres with part of it bordering the western side of the lake in March of 1890 he had a small hotel and some cottages built on the bluff overlooking the lake. By August of that year Jones decided to trade his farm and little resort for property in the town of Coloma with Dr. Wakeman Ryno, a Coloma physician. Dr. Ryno's use of the property was typical of that time period as he farmed part of the land, lived on part of the land, and rented out the lake frontage part of the land. Beside the cottages this area now known as Sylvan Heights became a popular picnic spot for church and fraternal groups to rent.

During that same year land development also started on the Watervliet side of Paw Paw Lake. In the October 24, 1890 issue of the <u>Watervliet Record,</u> it was reported that L. P. Husen (his story is told in Chapter 5) sold 15 lots in his Forest Beach subdivision and all these new owners said they intended to build cottages and make Paw Paw Lake their summer vacation destination. The success of Forest Beach as a resort subdivision was phenomenal. It seemed like everyone wanted property on the lake. By the 1890's part of the "American Dream" started to include a vacation at your summer cottage. After selling out Forest Beach, Husen moved on to start the next Watervliet lake side subdivision. In 1894 he purchased 17 acres of forest land with lake frontage and called it Beechwood Point. This property was broken into 130 lots to be sold for cottage sites, and one large piece of property was platted to be a hotel site within this resort subdivision.

Back on the Coloma side, Dr. W. A. Baker, a retired Coloma physician turned businessman, ran an advertisement in the <u>Coloma Courier</u>. This 1893 ad showed:

<u>Lots & Acreage</u>

4   ACRES   on **Williams Bay** for only **$240.00**

Also

1 ACRE on **Williams Bay $100** (Great place to build cottages)

In 1894 Chicago parties were reported to be negotiating for the purchase of Sylvan Heights, which had been part of the Ryno farm. In 1895 Sebastian Smith from Watervliet laid out 310 lots from part of his farm. Many of his lots on Pomona Point and the Outlet Bay had lake frontage. By 1899 A. J. Woodward decided to start providing entertainment for vacationers coming to the lake and proceeded to built a pavilion on part of the Woodward property.

The new century saw Paw Paw Lake land enter a booming period of rising values. Prices varied all over the lake for lake frontage lots. A lot in the year 1900 at Forest Beach went for $175.00 while a large lot in the same year at Beechwood Point sold for $1200.00. Beechwood Point on the Watervliet side of the lake was becoming known as the "Gold Coast."

THE RESORTER MAP.

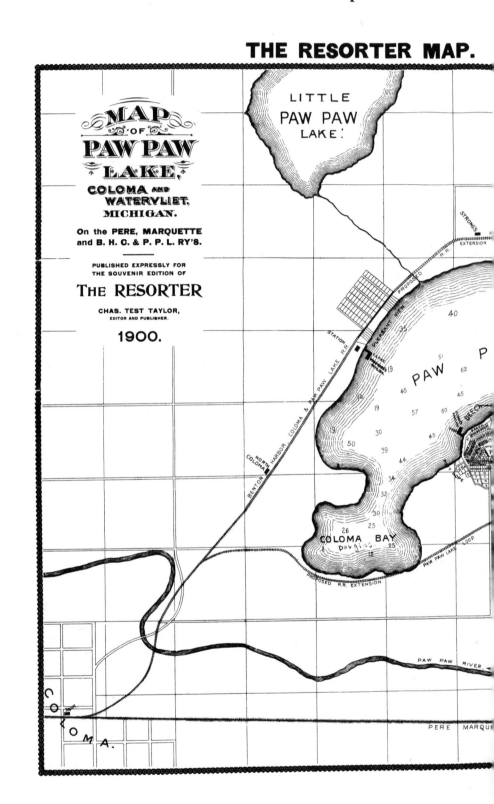

SOUVENIR EDITION 1900.

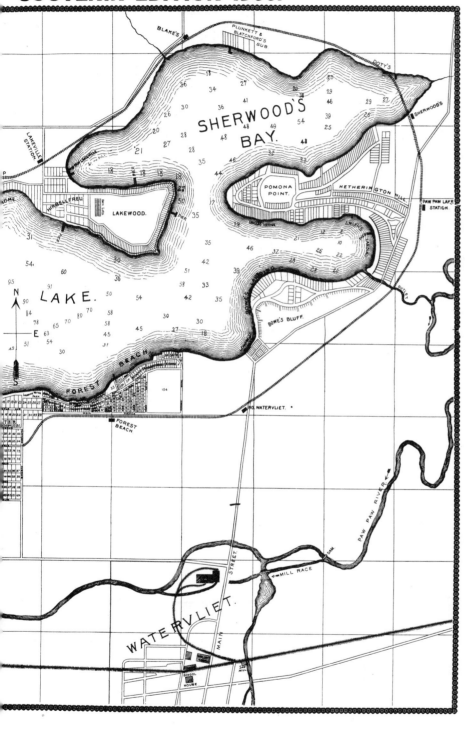

From A Newspaper called The Resorter in the year 1900.

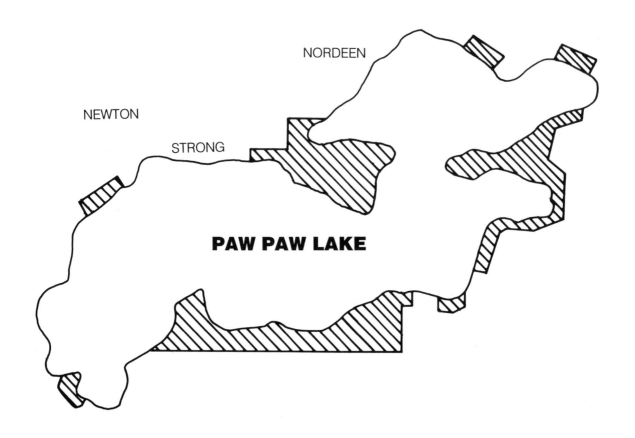

NORDEEN

NEWTON

STRONG

PAW PAW LAKE

The shaded areas taken from 1911 plat map of Paw Paw Lake

represent land subdivided into lots.

These shaded areas in the map above show the extent lake frontage was taken by developers as of 1911. The Watervliet side of the lake was the most developed for lots and cottages during this period. This side of Paw Paw Lake was considered the "in" area to have a cottage. Prices for lots were often much higher than anywhere else on the lake. If we include on the Coloma side the farmers turned resort owners (Newton, Strong, Nordeen,) it becomes evident that most of the lake frontage land was being used for resort purposes by that time.

THE LAND   Chapter 1

L. F. Boyer purchased a farm, part of it surrounding Douglas Bay, and proceeded to make it into Paw Paw Lake's first golf course. In 1917 he completed the first 9 holes at a cost of $1800.00 and opened with 47 members. By 1922 Boyer purchased additional land to complete the other 9 holes.

The roaring twenties brought the same kind of roaring action to property on and around Paw Paw Lake. Land and buildings changed hands, sometimes more than once in a year. Each property transaction seemed to be bigger than the last one. In 1922 property which had been owned by Sebastian Smith and his family since 1864 changed owners. This area on the Watervliet side, which had been called Pomona Point, was bought by Mr. and Mrs. A. F. Botto, who had it subdivided into 260 lots and called it Fairview. Property on the Coloma side of the Lake was also experiencing changes. These quotations from a story appeared in the 1925 Coloma Courier, as follows:

PAW PAW LAKE'S BIGGEST RESORT IS PURCHASED BY CHICAGO SYNDICATE

......*The biggest resort deal that has been closed in northern Berrien county in many years was the purchase of Alfred Nordeen's North Park Resort at Paw Paw Lake by C. Paul Talmadge, trustee for the North Park Community Resort Association.*

The Nordeen property at Paw Paw Lake was one of the largest resort properties on the Lake, with a water frontage of one-half mile. Included in the deal were all of the holdings of Mr. Nordeen. The farmland that was sold with the resort property consisted of about 87 acres and the resort property proper consisted of sixty-four platted lots and the land on which the hotel and other buildings were located. Some of the lake front lots had previously been sold. This property was formerly owned by the Williams interests of South Haven.

The North Park resort was purchased in the year 1908 by Alfred Nordeen, who came from Chicago, and has since made numerous improvements and greatly increased the value of his holdings. The hotel building of thirty rooms at that time stood on the opposite side of the road from its present location and adjoined the farm house, but two years ago the hotel

was moved to its present site and was remodeled. Besides the large hotel building there is one cottage that was included in this deal, besides laundry quarters and other necessary buildings. All of the farming equipment and the stock on the place was included in the sale.

While the purchasers of the property have not divulged all of their plans for the future, they have given out the information that a vast amount of money will be spent in making improvements on the place and converting it into a "community resort." The eighty-seven acres of farm land will be sub-divided and sold to a selected clientele of Chicago people and the land now occupied by the resort will be converted into a fine playground. It is the plan to erect a large number of new cottages during the coming season.

The 1920's witnessed the second boom of land development for the lake. It seemed like every piece of property was either for sale or just waiting to be redeveloped. Land was at a premium and could command top dollars. An example of this activity took place on the Coloma side in 1926. In 1925 a group of 41 lots on Benson Terrace fronting what was starting to be called Ellinee Bay, were put on sale for $6000.00. The summer of 1926 saw these same lots sell for $19,000.00. Paw Paw Lake as a resort destination, investment, or speculation venture rivaled any other lake in the Midwest.

Also in 1926 one of the last large unplatted tracts of land on Paw Paw Lake was bought. This 36 acres on Sherwood Bay would be called North Shore Highlands.

NORTHSHORE HIGHLANDS
ON
Paw Paw Lake Michigan

A Beautiful New Subdivision on State Trunkline Highway M-11 Near Watervliet Michigan

**NORTH SHORE HIGHLANDS
BEAUTIFULLY WOODED**

North Shore Highlands is a beautifully wooded tract of land situated on Sherwood Bay on the Northeastern shore of the lake about a mile from Watervliet.

Splendid large beech and maple trees form a canopy of leafy boughs high overhead. So that you can rest in their welcome shade and watch the fishermen on the lake or do any of the hundred and one things which you had planned to do when you had reached the woods.

As the name implies, the lots of North Shore Highlands are high and dry for cottage sites, and they are larger lots than you would expect in such a choice location. You can have all of the room you want ---for there is no need for your cottage to be jammed right up next to your neighbor's.

The lots on the lake front are of generous size, being wide and extending clear through from M-11 to the beach.

ORCHARD LOTS

The orchard lots are very high and afford an excellent view.

The apple trees on the orchard lots are in their prime and give promise of a good crop this season. So the fruit will not only be a welcome addition to the larder while here but also be a source of pleasure and profit when taken home and stored for the winter.

Nearby Hotels will serve meals to those of you who do not wish to be bothered with housekeeping and will provide additional accommodations for any guests.

Taken from a 1927 flyer given to the public for interested buyers.

THE LAND   Chapter 1

The 1920's ended fittingly with a development to top all of them. In 1929 George Klotter (his story is told in Chapter 5) announced his intention to develop some 700 acres of land and marshland into a series of islands and channels to be known as the "Venice of the North."

The beginning of the 1930's and the Depression started taking its effect on Paw Paw Lake. People continued to come each summer but not in as large of numbers nor did they stay for as long a time. No new developments or buildings were started. Some of the old hotels had few guests and some even stood vacant and boarded up. Property started to show up delinquent on the Berrien County tax roles. Land and buildings were being forfeited to the government because of back taxes. The county in turn would have public sales of the land and buildings for the taxes owed on it. At one point a lot at Paw Paw Lake could be bought for $52.87. A cottage on Bowes Landing could be rented for as little as $10.00 a month. The Great American Depression of the 1930's ended a 40-year span of land development and resort use around Paw Paw Lake.

During the Second World War there was little activity at the lake. Gasoline rationing stopped many people from making the trip for their summer vacation. There was no new construction because building materials were either scarce or non-existent having been taken for the war effort. By 1946 vacationers started returning but primarily to cottages they owned or rented. The great flood of 1947 further diminished any interest or desire for new building or uses of property surrounding the lake. In 1948 a six room cottage with 66 feet of lake frontage was being offered for as little as $3,720.00.

THE LAND   Chapter 1

The 1950's and 60's witnessed the next period of land use around the lake. During this time two developments in particular expressed the different directions lake property was headed. Cecil Potts, a local contractor, built and operated an outdoor animal zoo called Deer Forest Amusement Park.

This facility was the first of its kind in this part of the Midwest and soon became extremely popular with families locally and regionally. On summer weekends thousands of people would descend on Paw Paw Lake headed for Deer Forest. This influx of vacationers and their use of lodging and eating establishments helped keep a number of Paw Paw Lake businesses open that would have otherwise closed. The other change was the Paw Paw Islands. Curtis Coats had bought and finished what George Klotter had started a generation before. The historical significance of this development was the new way the property was marketed and sold. For the first time, lots on Paw Paw Lake were viewed as building sites for residential year round housing. The upscale housing and lake frontage prices in this development set a new level and direction for property on and around the lake.

The 1970's and 80's ushered in the next chapter of land use changes. In 1972, Bert M. Deaner took 22 acres of land on the Watervliet side (which was formerly Camp Achim - a Jewish boys camp) and started construction. However, instead of summer cottages, Deaner built A-frame style homes and advertised them for year-round rental. In 1975, on the Coloma side, a new phenomenon was taking place. Ted Drumm purchased part of what was once Strong's Resort property and began building and selling a new concept for Paw Paw Lake known as the "condominium." This was a new type of ownership of the land where buyers would own their units, but the property, buildings, and facilities were left in common ownership and maintained by paying a monthly assessment. In 1982 Larry McClanahan, a developer, built an 18 unit development called Lakeshore Condominiums on land which had been part of the original site of Woodward's Pavilion. By 1984 new developments were built on both sides of the lake. Sherwood Shores Condominiums was on the Watervliet side and Lake Pointe Condominiums was on the Coloma side. In 1985 Edgewater Condominiums was erected on part of the original Strong Farm. The advent of condominiums produced an ongoing dialogue and controversy over the use and direction of Paw Paw Lake property. By 1992 the Coloma Township side of the lake had enacted a ban on any new multi-building developments.

The years have brought many changes to the land around the lake. Where there were once orchards, subdivisions now stand. Pastures of land have given way to condominiums. In 1893 lake frontage property could be bought for 45 cents a foot. In 1993 the price is $1000 a foot. Depending on your point of view, these changes have been good or bad for the land. As we enter the next century, history will continue to alter and shape the land touching Paw Paw Lake.

Chapter 2

LAKEWOOD POINT

We have seen in the previous chapter, that as the use of Paw Paw Lake's waters changed so did the use of the surrounding lands. No longer was the cash crops logs or apples but rather vacationers. Land now had a resort value. To demonstrate this process, let us take Lakewood Point, one section of lake property and follow its development and uses through the years.

PAW PAW LAKE

In the early 1830's, Michigan was still part of the Northwest Territory. It did not become a state until 1837. In May of 1834, the U.S. government sold 70 acres of land bordering this lake to Stanford Buskirk. Physically, the land resembled a point, with lake frontage on three sides. Within three years Buskirk sold the land to Edward P. Deacon for $700.00 or $10.00 an acre. These first buyers were merely interested in the property as a real estate venture which could be turned over for a profit. For the next 45 years this piece of land changed owners numerous times, losing some of the acreage to other buyers through the years.

By the 1880's the southwestern area of Michigan was being settled more and more by people who wanted to farm the land. In 1882, a farmer and his wife, by the name of Charles J. and Mary E. Spenser, bought 47 acres which had become the total land area of Lakewood Point. They built a large farmhouse toward the end of the point. The Spensers cultivated a vineyard, raised cows, and logged the densely wooded point. In June of 1893, they officially lodged the first visitors to Paw Paw Lake and became one of the first farms to take in Chicago vacationers. In 1895 the Spensers were approached by a couple from Chicago who wished to purchase all 47 acres. Louis Felt, a Chicago business man, was interested in developing Spenser's Point into lots for vacationers. By the fall of that year they had settled on the price of $6500.00, and, in October, the land was sold to Louis and Esmerelda Felt. For the next couple of years, the Felts came out to the lake each summer and stayed in the big farmhouse as they had crews of men to clear and ready the land for development.

Toward the end of 1899 the Felts were ready to change the character of the Point forever.

> *Know all men by these presents that Louis W. Felt as proprietor and Esmeralda Felt his wife have caused the lands embraced in the annexed plat to be surveyed, laid out and platted to be known as LAKEWOOD and that the streets as shown on said plat are here by dedicated to the use of the public.*
>
> *The land embraced in the annexed plat of Lakewood is described as follows: Commencing on the shore of Paw Paw Lake at 1151 feet south and 697 feet east of the north quarter post of Section 15 town 3 south range 17 west, thence South 798 feet to shore of said lake thence easterly, northerly and westerly along the shore of said lake to the place of beginning.*

At 3:30 in the afternoon on November 11, 1899, the Register of Berrein County, Michigan, received and approved the plat and description for a subdivision to be called Lakewood.

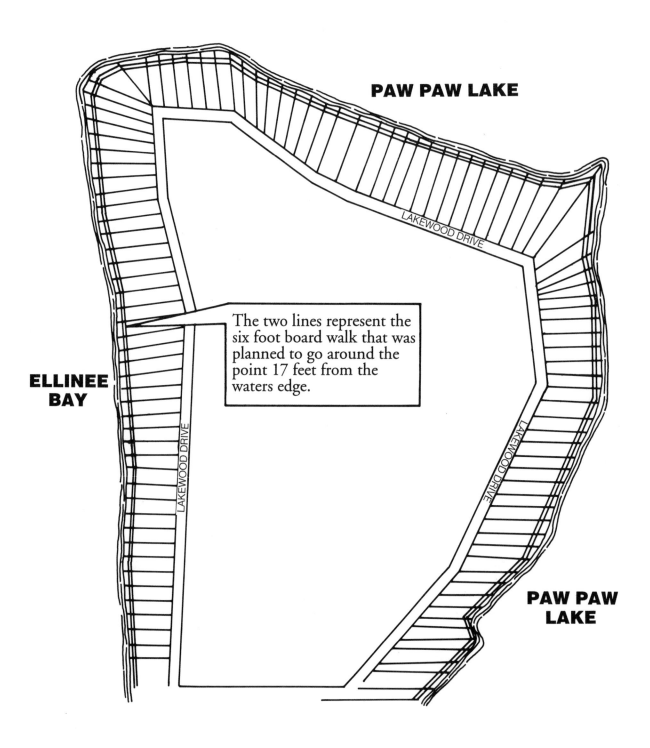

PAW PAW LAKE

LAKEWOOD DRIVE

The two lines represent the
six foot board walk that was
planned to go around the
point 17 feet from the
waters edge.

ELLINEE
BAY

LAKEWOOD DRIVE

LAKEWOOD DRIVE

PAW PAW
LAKE

A representation of the original lake lots on the Platt map of Lakewood Point

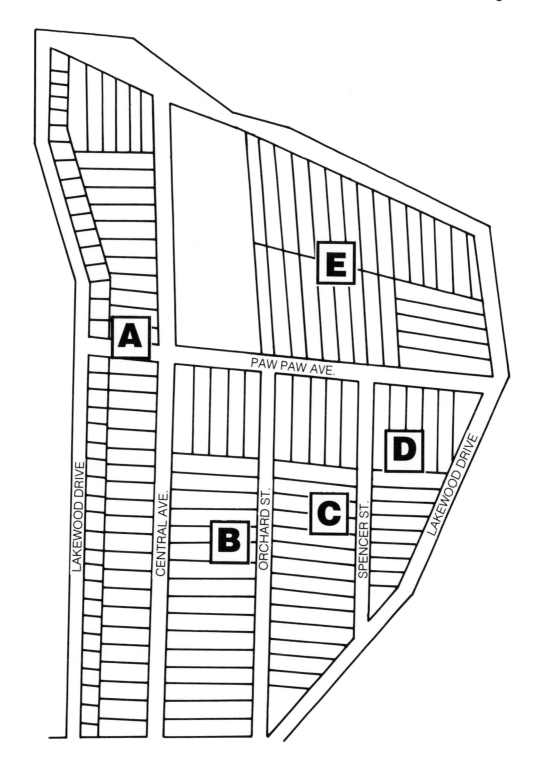

By 1901 Louis Felt subdivided into lots what was known as block 4 or the middle of the point.

LAKEWOOD POINT Chapter 2

Advertisements were placed in the Illinois and Michigan newspapers describing wonderful Paw Paw Lake and all the amenities Lakewood Point had to offer. Lake frontage lots were 40 feet wide and averaged 160 feet deep. They were being sold for $150.00 a lot. Property off the water was going for $75.00 a lot.

In the beginning, Lakewood Point lots sold at a slow pace. Initially the negatives of this location for vacationers outweighed the positives. The point was at the undeveloped end of the lake. The train from Coloma did not come out that far, and the road up the point was but a dirt path. Most of the lake lots were on a hill which met the need to build a stairway and having to walk up and down 30 to 40 feet to the shore. Another drawback was that the first couple of years of the century saw most of the "action" and building on the Watervliet side of the lake. Slowly the positives of this location did bring vacationers who wished to build cottages or stay at one of the resorts that had opened. The high ground meant no flooding and spectacular views of Paw Paw Lake. The remoteness gave people a true feeling of getting away from the city. Rail track was finally laid to a terminal at Baker's Bay, and resorters could now reach the point by train. By 1910, all of the lake frontage lots on Lakewood Point had been purchased.

One of the key forces that makes any development a success is word of mouth between groups of friends. The pleasures and benefits of Lakewood Point, Paw Paw Lake, Michigan, became the talk of two groups of Chicagoans. For a group of Swedish and Jewish southsiders Lakewood Point became the place to buy, build a cottage, or take a vacation at one of the resorts. The following two stories provide a sense of that history:

The spring of 1902 brought the widow, Rebecca Mayer and her two daughters, Bertha and Jennie, to the shores of Paw Paw Lake. This Jewish family came to check out land at Lakewood Point for a possible resort site. They liked the location, and on May 16, 1902, bought lots 5 and 6 for $195 from the developer Louis Felt. The sound of hammers and saws quickly filled the air as the family built the first cottages. By mid-summer of that year they were taking in their first group of Jewish vacationers from Chicago. Business was so good that they bought 3 more lots in 1903 and added more buildings. One of the buildings was known as the "Fun House" which became the entertainment center of the resort. Inside there was a piano, and people would come for sing alongs and skits. Each summer brought more and more people as word spread among the Jewish community back in Chicago about Lakewood Point. By 1910, this resort, called the Ravine, covered 9 lots and consisted of 7 buildings. The Ravine had become one of the largest Jewish resorts in the area. Bertha Mayer, the oldest daughter, managed the business end while Jennie took care of the kitchen and cooking. The mother ran a small convenience store from the front of her cottage.

The Ravine was successful for a number of reasons. First, it had become a well known and popular destination for not only families but also young Jewish people associated with some of the Chicago newspapers. Secondly, by not having a kosher kitchen, the atmosphere and attitude were casual and fun. Finally, there was little or no discrimination from the other owners or vacationers on Lakewood Point. The Mayer family continued to run the Ravine through the late 1920's when the daughters sold out to another Jewish businessman.

LAKEWOOD POINT   Chapter 2

In 1906 August Liljestrom, a Swedish southside building contractor, heard about Paw Paw Lake from another Swedish contractor friend. He decided to check it out as a possible summer retreat for his family. After walking around the whole lake and looking at various sites, Liljestrom decided to buy a number of lots on Lakewood Point and build a cottage on one of them. Through the years other relatives came up to visit, stay, and end up building their own cottages. In time these properties became a compound of six cottages filled with one big extended family. After hard surface roads were built from Illinois to Michigan, the Liljestrom family and relatives would travel to Paw Paw Lake by car. They would all rendezvous at a location on the southside of Chicago and as a caravan of cars, made the sometimes 10 to 15 hour drive to Paw Paw Lake. Each summer for years this Swedish clan would descend on Lakewood Point spending their days and nights enjoying all the pleasures Paw Paw Lake had to offer.

As in all families, the passage of time brought changes. Not everyone continued to come to Paw Paw Lake, but most kept some type of connection. In 1979, Genevive Sahlin, daughter of August Liljestrom and Phyllis Sahlin, granddaughter of August, decided to try to get some of the family back for a reunion. The call went out to return to Paw Paw Lake, and during one weekend in July one hundred and sixty people from nine states came back to once more share and enjoy the lake.

BOATS! BOATS! BOATS!
FOR RENT OR SALE

General Repair Work   Boat Builders
Johnson and Evinrude Motors
GEO. F. CONE BOAT CO.

Lakewood   Phone 4   Paw Paw Lake
Post Office --Coloma, Mich

BONELESS CAMP A. R. Linde, proprietor Coloma, Michigan.
Not stylish - For people who want to get away from dress, etc.

Home Cooking   Rates--$16 to $18 week: 3 day
TIPPECANOE RESORT

PAW PAW LAKE - COLOMA, MICH.

RICHARD PETERSON, PROP.

Located two blocks from Ellinee   Phone Coloma 24-w

Advertisements for three of the businesses on Lakewood Point in the 1920's

LAKEWOOD POINT Chapter 2

If we took a 1994 picture of Lakewood Point, it would reflect the changes Paw Paw Lake has made through the last 100 years. There are no longer any business establishments, hotels or boarding houses on Lakewood Point. Most of the Swedish and Jewish families are gone. Many of the homes have been winterized, and residents live there year round and the remaining cottages have been enlarged or remodeled. Except for a couple of lots, all of the lake frontage has been built on. Even though time has changed many things, it is evident that another generation continues the tradition of giving their time, money, and energy to Paw Paw Lake.

Chapter 3

RESORTS AND HOTELS

Even by today's standards, the speed of change for Paw Paw Lake is hard to imagine. Within a ten year period the lake went from having a handful of cottages to 50 hotels and over 600 cottages. The shift from an unknown and little used lake in a rural area, to a booming resort destination, personifies the American dream. This nation's diversity, ingenuity and drive were played out in the transformation of Paw Paw Lake.

This chapter captures a cross section of those events and changes over the last 100 years. We will see buildings, lifestyles, and attitudes reflected in the pictures, newspaper articles, and advertisements of this time period. By the late 1890's the number of vacationers coming to Paw Paw Lake was significant enough for the local newspapers to take notice. They realized that summer people represented a whole new market for increased circulation and advertising; consequently, these newspapers started reporting on the activities at the lake.

The following is taken from the *Paw Paw Lakelets* column of June 16, 1899 in the <u>Coloma Courier</u>. This social column would list the location, resort and some of the events taking place.

ISLAND PARK -

Chicago guests are at the Hotel Londeen for the summer.

FARM HOUSE -

Mrs. George Strong had guests for a number of weeks.

FOREST BEACH -

The Elm Dale house is overflowing with guests. The Lincoln cabin is the biggest and busiest little place along the whole north shore.

PLEASANT VIEW FARM -

Illinois vacationers are guests of Mrs. Mary M. Jenks for the summer.

EDGEWATER GLEN -

Captain Lyman Feltus' immense and elegant new clubhouse is approaching completion, and the building for the dining-room and kitchen is well along. The two soft water cisterns have a capacity of nearly one hundred and fifty barrels. Captain Feltus is also building a new steamer which will be sixty feet long by five feet breadth of beam. It is to be completed by July 1.

BEECHWOOD POINT -

An English family who are making a tour of the United States have decided to spend a few weeks at Paw Paw Lake and have taken a cottage here.

The Douglas View Resort

DR. P. E. DOUGLAS, Proprietor

The Douglas View Resort, with 800 feet of lake frontage on Douglas Bay, and several acres of woods, is one of the most popular stopping places for tourists visiting Paw Paw Lake.

This resort can accommodate 75 guests comfortably, and consists of several cottages and a spacious dining hall, all of which are situated over 30 feet above the lake, and a refreshment and boat house where all Paw Paw Lake steamers land.

The table is supplied with fruits, vegetables, etc., from farm run in connection with the resort. Pure drinking water is supplied from a deep, driven well, equipped with power, and attracts many visitors during the season from all parts of the lake. Rates, $7.00 per week; $1.50 per day. Take bus at Coloma for this resort. Address all communications to

F-9 on map   DR. P. E. DOUGLAS, Proprietor, Coloma P. O., Mich.

6

Tumblingrun Hotel

MRS. E. SELLS, Proprietor

Maplewood Station   P. O. Coloma, Mich.

A first-class resort on lake, with accommodations for forty-five guests. Only a few rods from fine dancing pavilion. First-class table. Fresh vegetables off the farm.

E-6 on map   Rates $7.00 and $8.00 per week—$1.50 per day

35

From a 1907 Resort Guide - Hotels on Coloma Side

Locust Beach

Pleasant View Station   Wooodward's Landing

C. L. NEWTON, Proprietor   Rates—$7 and $10 per week or $1.50 per day

A resort supplied with products from our own farm and dairy—with first class accommodations and spacious

F-4 on map   grounds.   Accommodations for 40 guests.

13

Strong's Station   **The Colonial**   Strong's Landing

A. HOCHSTADT, Proprietor

Accommo-
dations for
seventy
guests.

Rates—
$7.00 to $9.00
per week;
$1.50 per day.

Special attention paid to table   Fine Bathing Beach and Grounds

I-4 on map

26

From a 1907 Resort Guide - Hotels on Coloma Side

28

"Lincoln Cabin"

Forest Beach   P. O., Watervliet, Michigan

E. E. ROWLAND, Proprietor   Rates—$1.50 per day; $7 to $10 per week

Under the present management 10 years.

Indian goods   Curios
Souvenirs

Situate in the middle of Forest Beach about 20 feet above the level of the lake.   We have not all the modern conveniences, but if you go away hungry you are to blame.   If you don't sleep the bed is not at fault.

K-7 on map

34

Wigwam Hotel

"Catering to the Select"

5000 square feet of Verandas   Rates—$10.00 to $14.00 per week; $2.00 per day

Hotel, dining room and kitchen entirely under the supervision of women.   Home cooking and quiet, home-like surroundings absolutely assured.   Former guests our principal patrons.

I-7 on map

4

From a 1907 Resort Guide - Hotels on Watervliet Side

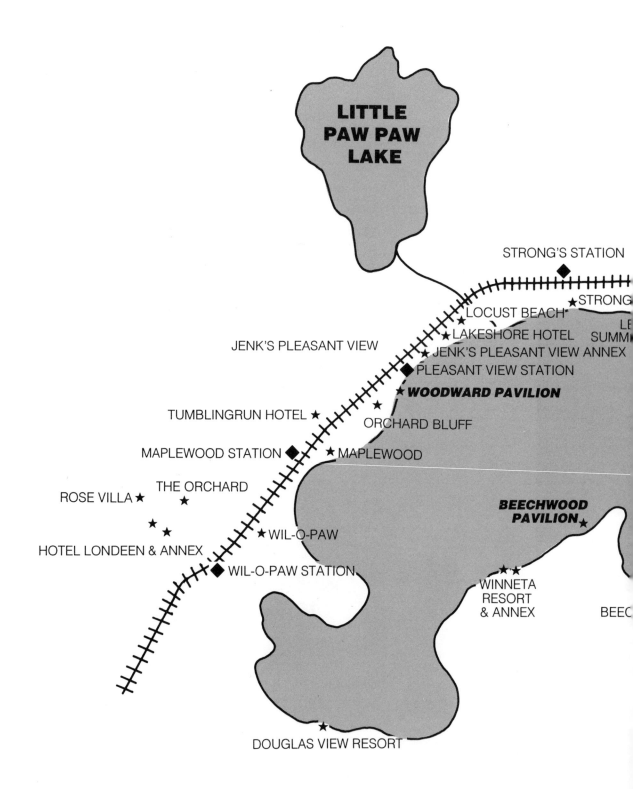

LITTLE
PAW PAW
LAKE

STRONG'S STATION

LOCUST BEACH

STRONG

LAKESHORE HOTEL

LE
SUMM

JENK'S PLEASANT VIEW

JENK'S PLEASANT VIEW ANNEX

PLEASANT VIEW STATION

WOODWARD PAVILION

TUMBLINGRUN HOTEL

ORCHARD BLUFF

MAPLEWOOD STATION

MAPLEWOOD

ROSE VILLA

THE ORCHARD

BEECHWOOD
PAVILION

HOTEL LONDEEN & ANNEX

WIL-O-PAW

WIL-O-PAW STATION

WINNETA
RESORT
& ANNEX

BEEC

DOUGLAS VIEW RESORT

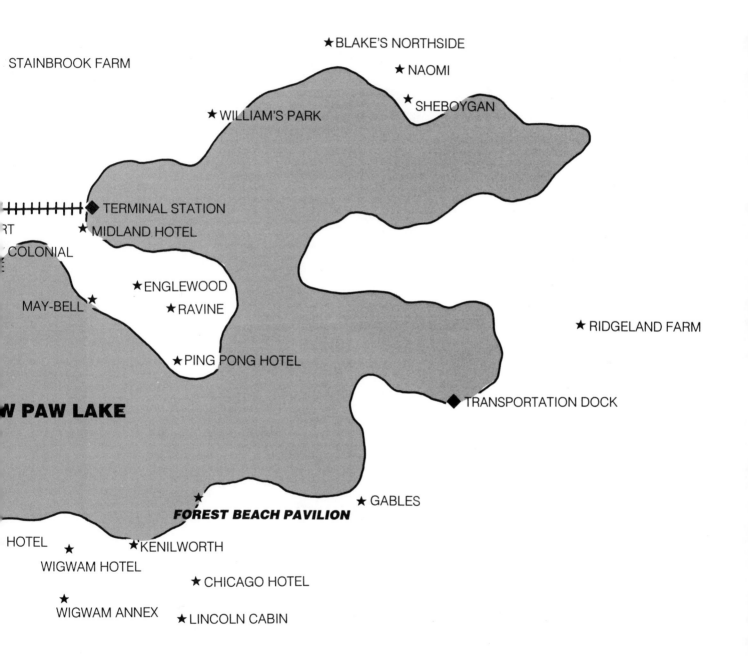

★ BRANCHWOOD

★ BLAKE'S NORTHSIDE

STAINBROOK FARM

★ NAOMI

★ SHEBOYGAN

★ WILLIAM'S PARK

◆ TERMINAL STATION

RT

★ MIDLAND HOTEL

COLONIAL

★ ENGLEWOOD

MAY-BELL ★

★ RAVINE

★ RIDGELAND FARM

★ PING PONG HOTEL

W PAW LAKE

◆ TRANSPORTATION DOCK

★

★ GABLES

FOREST BEACH PAVILION

HOTEL   ★   ★ KENILWORTH

WIGWAM HOTEL

★ CHICAGO HOTEL

★

WIGWAM ANNEX   ★ LINCOLN CABIN

From a 1907 Resort Guide about Paw Paw Lake.

Naomi Hotel
Windermere Pier (North Side)

L. ORMSBY, Manager   P. O. Coloma Mich.

Excellent
shade and
lawns.

Bathing
and
boating.

Situate on a beautiful bluff overlooking the lake.

First class table board.   Accommodations for ninety guests.   Rates $7.00

M-1 on map   to $9.00 per week; $1.50 per day.

8

Hotel Midland
Terminal Station

FRED SACHAU, Proprietor   Rates—$2 per day; $8 to $10 per week

Under new management; refurnished throughout; first class accommodations for 100 guests; unexcelled table-
board.   Situate at the water's edge with transportation by land or water at our door.

J-3 on map   An up-to-date establishment under experienced management.

17

From a 1907 Resort Guide - Hotels on Coloma Side

The Gables

Campbell's Breezyside   At the very water's edge   Accommodations for 35 guests

Fine Bathing Beach
Boating
and Fishing

Only 10 minutes
walk
to Watervliet

MRS. A. C. KING, P. O., Watervliet, Mich.   Terms—$1.50 per day; $7 and $8 per week

M-7 on map   All busses stop   First class accommodations

23

The Kenilworth
MRS. G. F. COLLETT, Prop.

P. O. and Railway Station, Watervliet   Kenilworth Landing

Rates $7.00 to $9.00 per week—$1.50 per day

A first-class resort with accommodations for fifty guests.   Excellent table board.

J-7 on map   On the water's edge.

33

From a 1907 Resort Guide - Hotels on Watervliet Side

RESORTS AND HOTELS   Chapter 3

The following is a description of some of the resorts from the 1926 Chicago Daily News Motor and Resort Guide.

BAY VIEW HOTEL, *O. A. Dodd, proprietor. Located right on the lake; bathing, dancing, horseback riding, moonlight boating and good home cooking. Write for rates. P.O. Watervliet, Michigan.*

THE FLORENCE HOTEL, *W. Henessy, proprietor, Coloma, Mich. On the north side of Lake. Excellent bathing beach. Convenient to all amusements and attractions. Home cooking. Free row boats.*

PLEASANT VIEW RESORT, *on Paw Paw Lake. Fishing, dancing, bathing, riding. Home cooking. Log bungalows for rent. Camp sites. Mrs. Etta McKay, R. 1., Coloma, Mich.*

STRONG'S RESORT, *Strong & Sons, proprietors, is on the north side of Paw Paw Lake, on stone road. It is an ideal lake hotel, with running water in the rooms. Boating, bathing, fishing, dancing and bowling near. Write for rates, Coloma, Mich.*

YE GOLFERS INN, *between two fairways, on the fine 18-hole championship golf course of the Paw Paw Lake Golf Club. Fine irrigated greens. The Inn and dormitory and cottages can accommodate golfers and other resorters. Moderate rates to desirable guests. Address: Paw Paw Lake Golf Club, Watervliet, Mich.*

THE WIGWAM stands on a charming spot on high ground flanked by massive trees and overlooking Paw Paw Lake. Mineral wells that furnish pure drinking water. Dancing at the Cottager's Country Club, only two blocks away. Golf at the Paw Paw Lake Golf Club, nearby, in consideration of a small fee. Fishing, bathing, bowling, billiards. Watervliet, Mich, F.F. Gross, proprietor.

RESORTS AND HOTELS   Chapter 3

In 1929 the Coloma Chamber of Commerce and the Watervliet Record listed accommodations:

Coloma Side

Colonial Hotel - 75 people
Mrs. S.P. Cone - 5 cottages
Bert Cooper - 2 cottages
Crystal Place Annex - 25 people (rooms only)
Berky's Villa - 80 people
Doris Hotel - 30 people
Douglas View - 4 cottages
Englewood Hotel - 25 people
Florence Hotel - 75 people
Genoar's Resort - 40 people
Gillice Hotel - 125 people
Green Lantern Inn - 20 people and one cottage
Hyde Park Hotel - 10 people and one cottage
Kent Cottages - 5
Albert Kibler - 12 people and 1 cottage
Lakeside Resort - 30 people
Lake View Hotel - 15 people
Lakewood Hotel - 60 people

Lampson's Resort - 30 people
Liberman's Resort - 30 people
Locust Beach Resort - 50 people.
Maplewood Hotel - 50
Naomi Hotel - 50 people
North Park Resort - 125 people
Orchard Inn - 75 people
Paw Paw Inn - 40 people
Ravine Hotel - 90 people
Rose Cottages - 5 cottages
Shoreland Hotel - 30 people
L.D. Stout - 5 cottages
Strejc's Resort - 50 people
Strong's Resort - 125 people 1 cottage
Tippecanoe Hotel - 50 people
Woodward's Hotel - 200 people
Ye Aelyse Lou - 6 people

Watervliet Side

Bayview Hotel
Belmont Hotel
Chicago Hotel
Commodore Hotel
Delmont Hotel
Gerbers Hotel
The Hermitage Hotel
Kenilworth Hotel
Lincoln Cabin
Pokagon Hotel
Wigwam
Ye Golfers Inn

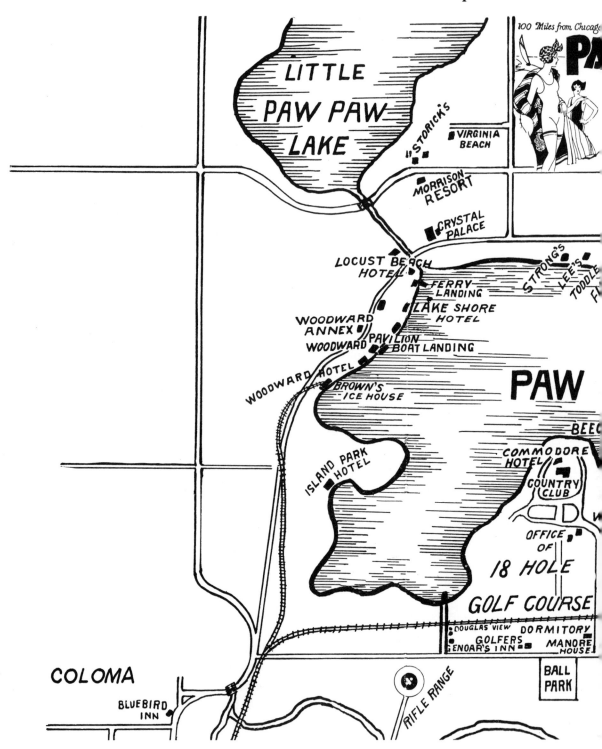

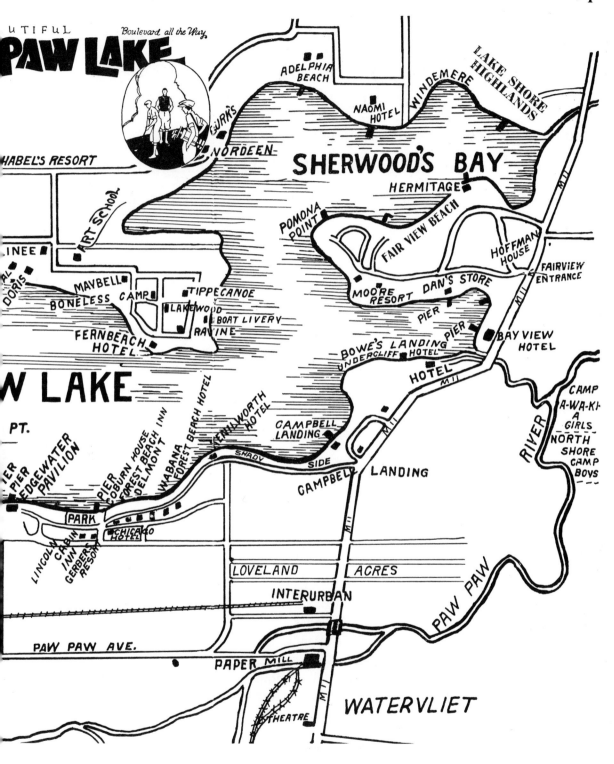

UTIFUL
PAW LAKE   *Boulevard all the Way*

HABEL'S RESORT

ART SCHOOL

ADELPHIA BEACH

BURK'S

NORDEEN

NAOMI HOTEL

WINDEMERE

LAKE SHORE HIGHLANDS

SHERWOOD'S BAY

HERMITAGE

POMONA POINT

FAIR VIEW BEACH

HOFFMAN HOUSE

FAIRVIEW ENTRANCE

INEE

DORIS

MAYBELL

BONELESS CAMP

TIPPECANOE

LAKEWOOD

FERNBEACH HOTEL

BOAT LIVERY

RAVINE

MOORE RESORT   DAN'S STORE

PIER

W LAKE

PT.

PIER

EDGEWATER PAVILION

PIER

COBURN HOUSE

FOREST BEACH INN

DELMONT

WABANA

FOREST BEACH HOTEL

KENILWORTH HOTEL

CAMPBELL LANDING

SHADY

SIDE

BOWE'S LANDING

UNDERCLIFF HOTEL

HOTEL

PIER

BAY VIEW HOTEL

RIVER

CAMP A-WA-KI-A GIRLS

NORTH SHORE CAMP BOYS

PARK

CHICAGO HOTEL

LINCOLN

CABIN INN

GERBER'S RESORT

CAMPBELL   LANDING

LOVELAND   ACRES

INTERURBAN

PAW PAW AVE.

PAPER MILL

THEATRE

PAW PAW

WATERVLIET

A 1927 Map of Paw Paw Lake.

RESORTS AND HOTELS

This is a partial list from a 1936 flyer for both the Coloma and Watervliet sides of the lake. By this period there is a noticeable change in the accommodations being offered to the vacationers. This shift of more cottages being available, was due to the increase of families driving their cars to Paw Paw Lake for their vacation. The three tourist camps that are listed are in fact early motels.

HOTELS

Bay View Hotel	Naomi Hotel	Shoreland Hotel
Betty's Hotel	North Park Hotel Resort	Strejc Hotel
Fair View Inn Hotel	Pokagon Hotel	Strong's Hotel
Gerber's Hotel	Rattrays Hotel	Wabana Inn Hotel
Maplewood Hotel	Sherman Hotel	

COTTAGES

Berkey's Cottages	Fisher's Cottages	Ravine Cottages
Berkley's Cottages	Florence Cottages	Real's Cottages
Betty's Cottages	Gillice Cottages	Rose Cottages
Burke's Hollywood Cottages	Holland Cottages	Sadowski Cottages
Campbell's Cottages	Kibler's Cottages	Schwarting Cottages
Colonial Cottages	King's Cottages	Shamrock Cottages
Cooper's Cottages	Leslie's Cottages	Stout's Cottages
Cross Cottage	McMullen's Cottagess	Strong's Cottages
Crystal Place Cottages	Paw Paw Lake Camp	Vollrath Cottages
Dellwood Cottages	Pleasant View Cottages	Werner's Cottages
Douglas View Cottages		

TOURIST CAMPS

Carp's Court	Chet's Motor Lodge	Paw Paw Lake Camp

RESORTS AND HOTELS

The 1940's hastened the end of the golden era for the resorts and hotels around Paw Paw Lake. The war years of 1941 through 1945 saw some establishments not even open for the season or only on a limited basis. After the war this pattern of half capacity for many of the resorts continued to plague owners. Some owners sensing this trend decided to get out of the summer vacation business. A few tried to winterized their cottages and started renting them to local people as year round rental property. By the 1950's vacationers were still coming to the lake but in smaller numbers. This change in vacation destination and lifestyle was in fact happening all over America. With interstate roads and reasonable plane fares, the public wanted to see more than just Paw Paw Lake anymore.

A few places like Strong's Resort, tried to keep the old traditions alive. Here was a place the family could stay and never leave the grounds if they so desired. Chicago families would coordinate their vacations with each other so that they could meet at Strong's and vacation at the same time. People would renew friendships from years gone by for a weekend or a week once a year. The skits, the songs, and the campfires gave everyone a common bond and feeling of community. Most of the vacationers took the "American plan" which meant taking your meals in the big dinning room with everyone else. A large bell would be rung calling everyone to mealtime. Once seated, everyone would participate in family style, passing the huge quantities of food around the table. Mrs. Catherine Strong took pride in making and providing the best food to be found at Paw Paw Lake. This type of vacation and way of life which had been the norm for many years, was soon to become only a memory around Paw Paw Lake.

As this list from the 1960's demonstrates, fewer than 1/3rd of all the hotels and resorts were left by that time period. Changing lifestyles for vacationers had finally taken its toll on Paw Paw Lake.

MOTELS

BUENA VISTA MOTEL

Watervliet, Michigan-on U.S. 12--2 miles East Watervliet and 4 miles East Coloma--Kitchenette and TV--Open All year.

CHEZ DU LAC MOTEL

Modern Motel and Kitchenette Units--Beauty-rest equipped. Private, Sandy Beach, Boating, Fishing, Lawn Games, Write or Call Irwin Surland, R. 4, Box 302, Coloma, Michigan.

FOREST VIEW MOTEL

All New, Spacious Units, TV, Picnic Grounds with Play Area. Right next to Deer Forest. Write for Reservations to Wm. Semand, Coloma, Michigan.

PAW PAW LAKE MOTOR LODGE

Forest Beach Road--Watervliet, Michigan--Modern Kitchenette Apartments-Tiled Showers--Swimming Pool--Shuffle-board--Barbecue Pits and Picnic Facilities. Hans Briese, Prop.

SCHICK'S MOTEL

Deluxe Motel Units and Housekeeping Cottages--Tiled Showers, TV available, Beauty rest-equipped--Private Sandy Beach and 80-ft. Dock for your Boating Pleasure. Write or call: R. 4, Box 156, Coloma, Michigan.

WETZEL'S MOTEL

Clean Modern Rooms--Beauty-rest equipped. New Kitchenettes--Beach Privileges. Owned and operated by Della Greiffendorf, R. 4, Box 63, Coloma, Mich.

COTTAGES

BILLY BERK'S NEW LOG CABINS

All modern Units--Kitchenettes--Boating--Fishing--Swimming Near Club Rocadero--Paw Paw Lake--Write or Phone, Coloma, Michigan, R. 4, Box 410.

IVY DELL

Modern Two-bedroom, Lake Front Cottages with Showers, Private Beach--Boats Furnished--Write or Call Martha Bishop, R. 4, Box 427, Coloma, Mich.

KENDALL'S COTTAGES & GROCERIES

Modern Housekeeping Cottages--Located 1 block from Deer Forest--Play Area for Children--R. 4, Box 158, Coloma, Mich.

MARTIN'S COTTAGES

Modern 1 and 2 Bedroom Cottages--Private Beach--Boats Furnished--Write or Call Cecil Martin, Coloma, Mich., R. 4, Box 297.

McCREA'S ROSE COTTAGES

Cottages and Apartments--Private--Safe, Sandy Beach. R. 4, Box 157A, Coloma, Mich.

MOTTO'S ROYAL COTTAGES

Equipped with modern conveniences--Also Spacious Grounds and Private Beach for your family's vacation pleasures. Write R. 4, Box 170, Coloma, Michigan.

COTTAGES (continued)

WOODY'S COTTAGES

Modern Two-bedroom-Private Beach-Boats Furnished. Write, R. Woodhams, Lakewood Point, R. 4, Box 386, Coloma, Michigan.

ZERBE'S COTTAGES

Modern Cottages with Bath and Showers--Private Sandy Beach--Pier-Fishing--Spacious Grounds--L. Zerbe, R. 4, Box 153, Coloma, Michigan.

HUGHES COTTAGES

Light Housekeeping 1-2-3 Bedroom Cottages--Tourist Rooms Beach--Boating--Reasonable rates--Write or Call: Coloma, Mich., R. 4, Box 282, Florence Hughes.

RESORTS

BETTY'S RESORT

Modern Hotel Rooms and Cottages w/baths. Ideal Family Resort--Located in center of many activities. Mrs E. Elias, Paw Paw Lake, R. 4, Box 281, Coloma, Michigan.

BROWN VIEW LODGE

Private Beach, Sun Pier--All modern conveniences on Greyhound bus line--Reservation required Florence G. Brown owner. R. 4, Box 305.

DELLWOOD RESORT

Light Housekeeping Cottages-Spacious Grounds Beach Privileges--Reasonable Rates--Restaurant on Premises. Tel. or Write: R. 4, Box 292, Coloma, Michigan.

LAKECREST RESORT

Modern Housekeeping Cottages--Apartments--Hotel Accommodations--Centrally Located--Showers--Private Beach on Lake--Picnic Area--Barbecue Pits--Boats Bicycles--Pavilion with Soda Bar--Coloma, Michigan, R. 4, Box 284.

RESORTS (continued)

LOVELY'S LODGE

Offers complete vacation lodging--including rooms and modern housekeeping Cottages with or without meals--Spacious Grounds--Private Beach Privileges--Reasonable Rates. For Reservations call Coloma, Mich., R. 4. Box 160, Coloma, Michigan.

MAPLEWOOD RESORT

First Stop on Paw Paw Lake--Modern, and Apartments--Gas Heat--Private, Safe, Sandy Beach 60 ft. Pier--Ample Parking near all Amusements. R. 4, Box 145, Coloma, Michigan.

MARIMAC RESORT

All Modern 2-bedroom Cottages--Electric Refrigeration.Showers--TV--BoatsFurnished--Private Sandy Beach on Beautiful Little Paw Paw Lake--R. 4, Box 506, Coloma, Michigan.--M. Hanson, Proprietor.

OASIS RESORT

Modern Housekeeping Motel Apartments--Private Showers, Beach Facilities--Located near all Activities--Write or Call R. 4, Box 283, Coloma, Michigan - R. Nicolais, Prop.

PAW PAW ISLE RESORT

Modern Two-bedroom Apartments--Electric Refrigeration, Gas Heat--Private Beach--60 foot Pier. D. Kliger, R. 4, Box 85A, Coloma, Michigan.

REAL'S RESORT

Modern Housekeeping Motel Apartments--Privileges--Bate Fishing Equipment--Outboard or Rowboats for Rent. R. 4, Box 167, Coloma, Michigan.

STRONG'S RESORT

The Friendly Family Resort on Paw Paw Lake that pleases you. Rooms--Cottages and Apartments Available--Restaurant on Premises. Write Strong & Sons, c/o Strong's Resort, R. 4, Box 278, Coloma, Mich.

41

By 1994 only two resorts on the Coloma side still exist with lake frontage to take in vacationers. They continue to represent and carry on a 100 year tradition.

Chapter 4

TRANSPORTATION

During Paw Paw Lake's peak years as a resort destination, over 50,000 people came to the lake each summer. How did that many people make their way to a lake in rural Michigan? The answer to this question shows not only why Paw Paw Lake became so successful, but also demonstrates America's progress in the technology of transportation. From a couple young men walking all the way from Chicago, to a man landing his bi-plane on the lake and taxing up to his cottage, people have make their way to Paw Paw Lake.

Let us go back and take a hypothetical family from 1894 and trace their journey. This Chicago family would rise very early in the morning and take several street cars to the docks on Lake Michigan. There they would take a steamship for the 4 1/2 hour trip to Benton Harbor, Michigan. The family would then take seats on a horse drawn wagon for the trip to Coloma or Watervliet. At this point they would transfer to a smaller wagon or buggy for the ride to Paw Paw Lake. They would then board a boat which would take them to one of the hotels or resorts on the lake finally completing their journey.

Graham & Morton
LINE
St. Joseph and Benton Harbor Division

Operating the only line of large, steel side-wheel Steamers on Lake Michigan

All Steamers connect with special train for Paw Paw Lake to and from, and with Pere Marquette, Michigan Central, and C. C. C. & St. L. Steam Railroads, also with Southern Michigan Interurburen, and Benton Harbor & Eau Claire Interurban Electric Railways at St. Joseph and Benton Harbor.

"CITY OF BENTON HARBOR" and **"CITY OF CHICAGO"**

Summer Schedule, Effective June 22, '07

LEAVE CHICAGO 9:30 A. M., Week days only—50c Rd Trip—Arrv. St Joe 1:30 P. M.

LEAVE CHICAGO 12:30 Noon, Mon., Wed., and Fri. - 50c Rd Trip. This is a continuous Round Trip Excursion, simply changing steamers at St. Joseph and arriving back in Chicago at 9:00 P. M.

LEAVE CHICAGO 2:00 P. M., Saturday only—50c each way—Arrv. St. Joe, 6:00 P. M.

LEAVE CHICAGO 10:00 A. M., Sunday—50c each way, $1.00 Rd Trip - Arrv. St. Joe 2:00 P. M.

LEAVE CHICAGO 11:30 Every Night—50c each way, $1.00 Rd Trip—Arrv. St. Joe 3:30 A. M.

LEAVE BENTON HARBOR 7:00 A. M. Monday, Wednesday, Friday and Saturday only—Arrv. Chicago 11:30 A. M.

LEAVE BENTON HARBOR 3:30 and 8:30 P. M. Week days—Arrv. Chicago 9:00 P. M. and 3:00 A. M.

LEAVE ST. JOSEPH 7:30 A. M. Monday, Wednesday, Friday and Saturday only—Arrv. Chicago 11:30 A. M.

LEAVE ST. JOSEPH 5:00 and 10:30 P. M. Week days—Arrv. Chicago 9:00 P. M. and 3:00 A. M.

LEAVE ST. JOSEPH 6:00 and 10:30 P. M. Sunday—Arrv. Chicago 10:00 P. M. and 3:00 A. M.

FROM CHICAGO	One Way	Round Trip
Berrien Springs	$0.80	$1.50
Niles, Mich	.95	1.75
South Bend, Ind	1.15	2.00
Paw Paw Lake		1.75

Meals and Berth Extra. Berth Rates, entire Stateroom, $1.75. Lower Berth, $1.00. Upper Berth, 75c. Meals. 50c. This company reserves the right to change this schedule without notice.

For General Information--Main Office, Benton Harbor, Michigan
Phone Twin City No. 113--Bell No. 4, 2 rings

Chicago Dock, Foot Wabash Avenue
Telephone Central 2162

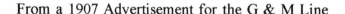

From a 1907 Advertisement for the G & M Line

This boat from the Graham and Morton Ship Company and other boat lines brought over tens of thousands of people each summer. Vacationers would embark at the docks in Chicago and disembark at St. Joseph and Benton Harbor. A number of these boats could accommodate up to two thousand people. Many would then continue on to Paw Paw Lake. During the early part of the century there were numerous newspaper reports about people being stranded at the dock because that ship departing was full. They would then have to wait for the next boat to leave. This popular and fun means of transportation to Michigan continued through the 1940's.

Two steamships, from different time periods, City of Benton Harbor and S.S. Theodore Roosevelt, arriving at the St. Joseph River.

Greetings from Paw Paw Lake, Mich.
Smiths Landing.

A 1909 Postcard showing the Steamboat The Margaret.

The photograph above shows the steamboat, the "Margaret" docking at Smith's Landing with a load of vacationers. This boat had been built for Captain Lyman Feltus at the turn of the century. He named it in honor of his daughter. It was one of the largest boats on the Lake, measuring 88 feet long and 22 feet wide. This steamboat had room for a piano and could accommodate up to 125 people. The other large boat, similar to the "Margaret" was called the "City of Paw Paw Lake" and could take 200 passengers. These boats served two functions. First, they would pick up passengers from the trains and take them by water to their hotels. Secondly, they would give people a ride to the various pavilions and other entertainment around the lake.

Two of the smaller boats on the lake the "Gypsy" and the "Favorite."

TRANSPORTATION   Chapter 4

CHICAGO & WEST MICHIGAN RAILROAD

SOUTHERN MICHIGAN RAILROAD

PERE MARQUETTE RAILWAY

BENTON HARBOR & ST. JOSEPH RAILWAY & LIGHT CO.

CHICAGO SOUTH SHORE & SOUTH BEND RAILROAD

CHESAPEAKE AND OHIO RAILROAD

AMTRACK RAILROAD

Each one of these railroad lines over the last century played its part in bringing people to this area. Just as trains opened the United States to development, they had the same effect for Paw Paw Lake. Here was an inexpensive method of transportation which was able to bring vacationers by the thousands almost to the shores of Paw Paw Lake.

Even though the trains came to Coloma and Watervliet, there was seen a need to bring a train all the way to the lake. Dr. W. A. Baker of Coloma organized a company, and by 1896, had built the first train and track to Pleasant View Station at Paw Paw Lake. Within a short period, the train was continued on as far as Williams Park with stops at Strong's Resort and the terminal station at Baker's Bay. This method of travel to the lake also had the effect of closing a number of livery companies in Coloma for lack of passengers. Very quickly this became the most popular means of reaching the lake. In that first summer of 1896, 14,000 thousand passengers were recorded to have taken the train. By the year 1900 there were 40,000 passengers.

THE NEW INTERURBAN TO PAW PAW LAKE

One of the sources for train travel at the start of the 20th century took this nation by storm. This "interurban" or what we would call today an electric train or trolley became one of the solutions to America needs in transportation. It was fast and relatively easy to build and could go anywhere. By 1917 there was a network of over 18,000 miles of track, where 20 years before there had been nothing. The flat terrain of the Midwest was ideal for this system to grow and multiply. This "interurban" system wasn't going to replace the steam trains but rather go everywhere they didn't go. It would connect the rural areas and cities as never before. Small towns and smaller villages competed with each other to get the interurban to come to their territory.

TRANSPORTATION   Chapter 4

Coloma and Watervliet were no different in wanting "Progress" to come to their communities. Even though it would be years before it came, this excerpt of an editorial from The Coloma Courier in 1893 sets the tone with its flowery boosterism for the need of the interurban.

An electric horse streetcar railroad must be built from this village to Benton Harbor. The vast and annually increasing harvests of small fruits and other products in this immediate vicinity demand it. The growing fame of this village and Paw Paw Lake, whose blue and beautiful expanse has so long lain sleeping in the summer sun awaiting the coming of the sick and weary denizens of the overcrowded cities, demand it. The fair and perhaps fabulous profits to the stock-holders of so needful an enterprise, who would be largely the fruit-growers and farmers and gardeners for a mile-wide swath on both sides of the line, demand it. When a cargo of Chicago men, women and little children learn that they can so cheaply reach so beautiful a little inland, see as Paw Paw Lake, and hang their hammocks from the firm limbs of the native forest trees that grow to the very water's edge, can sail or row their boats upon its surface and bathe in it's liquid depths, or romp over the swelling hills, and climb the fences, tear their clothes, and blister their hands and feet in the wild woods along the shore or not far away, and have the freest and jolliest and most untrammeled day or week or summer they can find this side of Lake Michigan, they will never remain a day in our seaport towns, but take the first car for Coloma. The road must and shall be built!

By 1912 the interurban had come to Coloma, Watervliet, and both sides of Paw Paw Lake. These trains out to the lake also precipitated some of the boat lines to go out of business. For the first time in history a person could take a train from anywhere in the Midwest and reach Paw Paw Lake.

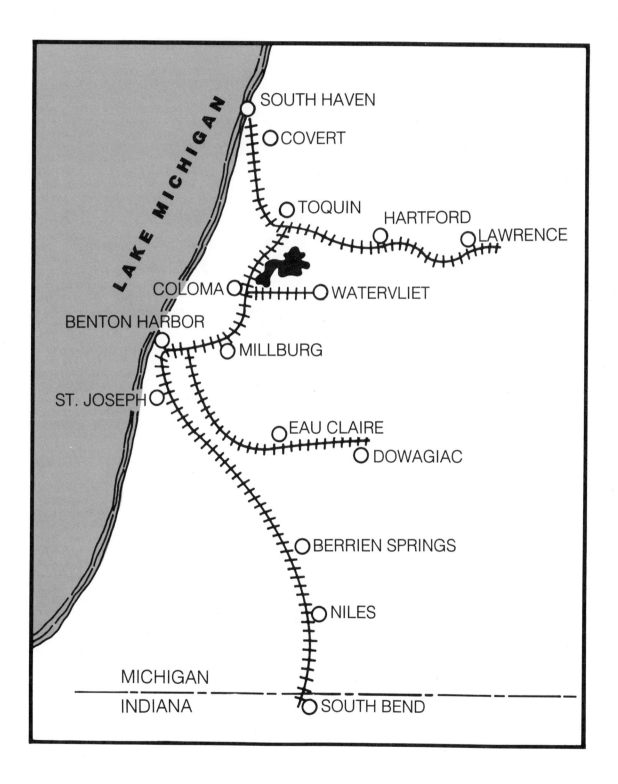

A map of the interurban lines around 1915 in Southwestern Michigan

TRANSPORTATION

Chapter 4

A proud Chicago family in their Abbott-Detroit automobile at their cottage on Paw Paw Lake around 1916. (Notice the right hand steering wheel)

The last method of transportation to arrive at Paw Paw Lake was the automobile. The first car reported to come to Coloma was in 1907. By the beginning of World War I hundreds of cars were making their way to Paw Paw Lake each summer. In fact by the summer of 1917 the Berrien County Sheriff had declared war on all speeders driving in the county and would arrest anyone going over the 25 mile an hour speed limit. The 1920's saw this new form of transportation proceed to make the interurban lines to the lake obsolete. From the 1930's to the present time, cars have become the primary method of reaching Paw Paw Lake.

"GREYHOUND" MOTOR COACH SERVICE IN WESTERN MICHIGAN

The Safety Motor Coach Lines of Muskegon operate seventy-five big, luxurious, blue "Greyhounds" over an extensive route from Chicago to Ludington and all intervening points.

During the summer months Greyhounds will run hourly from Chicago to all of Western Michigan resorts as far north as Ludington and as far west as Grand Rapids.

The Greyhounds began operation a year and a half ago with the run between Muskegon and Grand Rapids, where hourly service is maintained the year round, and over night gained the envied popularity of being the best, quickest, most frequent and comfortable made of inter-city travel. Today the word "Greyhound" in this section of the country is a household word on the lips of everyone, and stands for the best in motor coach travel that Western Michigan has ever enjoyed.

Each coach is beautifully upholstered and equipped with individual, air-cushioned arm chairs, immaculately clean and piloted by expert drivers. Nothing has been spared in the way of equipment or service to make the "Greyhounds" the last word in motor coach travel and today enjoy the reputation of being America's model coach line.

Taken from a mid 1920's advertisement describing bus travel.

At the same time the automobile was becoming the predominant mode of transportation, the motor coach came into existence. These motor coaches as they were first called were a natural extension of the automobile. Local bus lines started serving the same purpose as the horse and wagon had done for previous generations. It was not long before many of these smaller lines were bought out and consolidated into a larger system. This system in Western Michigan became the Greyhound Bus Line.

Scenic Beauty all the way

Western Michigan is a happy hunting ground for lovers of Nature and through this scenic country M-11 winds its way along Lake Michigan, taking in scores of cities, towns, villages and resorts. The lure of the great Outdoors and the charm of the smooth open road are made doubly attractive by Greyhound Parlor Coaches operating on frequent punctual schedules throughout the Playground of the Nation.

"Ride the Greyhounds"

CIRCLE $1 TOUR

Paw Paw Lake

40-MILE SCENIC ROUTE

Daily Tour leaving Benton Harbor at 1:15 upon arrival of Excursion Boat from Chicago. A fascinating 40-mile Scenic Ride in a comfortable Greyhound Parlor Coach. Tickets on Goodrich Boats and at Benton Harbor Greyhound Station.

Taken from a 1927 summer time schedule for the Safety Motor Coach Lines

Chapter 5

MOVERS AND SHAKERS

This chapter is for all those "Movers and Shakers" through the years who gave their dreams, energy, and money to make Paw Paw Lake a success. Many of the early developers accomplishments have become only memories or forgotten by time.

I have chosen five men not as well known but who demonstrate and personify the spirit which made Paw Paw Lake. Each one of these gentlemen played a part and influenced the history of Paw Paw Lake.

The Civil War Veteran

The Ship Builder

The Jeweler

The Inventor

The Realtor

THE CIVIL WAR VETERAN

Prosper O. Bowe was born in 1842 in Clayton, New York. His father, Horace Bowe, a farmer, settled in Bainbridge Township, Berrien County, Michigan, in 1855. Bowe grew up on the family farm learning the ways of the land and animals. With his 18th birthday came the start of or nation's Civil War. In October of 1861, Bowe enlisted in the union army. Like thousands of other young men, he volunteered because of patriotism and adventure. Like most, he also thought his duty would only last 6 months to a year. Bowe stayed in the army through the end of the war in 1865.

During the war he was a member of Company D from Michigan which was attached to the famous 66th Illinois Sharp Shooters and participated in some of the major battles of the Civil War. Bowe ended the war with the Georgia Campaign and was with General Sherman on his march to the sea. Since the army did not pay very much, the United States government had the custom of giving bonuses to men who fought in battles. Grateful state and local governments or other groups also provided monetary bonuses. Consequently, with the long list of battles Bowe had been in, he came home a monetarily well off veteran of the Civil War.

He quickly became one of the more prominent men in Berrien County. He purchased a large tract of land with part of it adjoining the Paw Paw River and Paw Paw Lake. Bowe devoted much of his energy to dairy farming and raising cattle. He was also interested in the growth and prosperity of the town of Watervliet. He helped start the first canning factory in town, was an officer in the Watervliet Creamery Company and a stock holder in the Watervliet Paper Company. As Paw Paw Lake started to change its character Bowe was one of its pioneer developers. He was one of the first to have his lake frontage platted and leased the land for resorters' cottages.

His home overlooking Paw Paw Lake, was the site for his other love and joy in life, reunions of his beloved Company D. For 25 years his comrades of Company D from the Grand Army of the Republic held their annual reunions on his farm and lake property. This encampment and the many activities would last a number of days and became one of the highlights of summers at the lake. Bowe died at the age of 81 in 1923. His life and commitment to his community are an example of the finest qualities to be found in the men who made Paw Paw Lake's history.

THE SHIP BUILDER

Henry Waterman Williams was born in Burlington, Vermont, in 1829. He grew up there and became a ship carpenter by trade. At the age of 22, Henry built the first transfer boat ever used in the United States. This vessel was 44 feet wide and 350 feet long. This boat was used by the Vermont Central Railroad to transfer merchandise in car lots across Lake Champlain to New York state and back to Vermont. By 1852 Williams had become a wealthy man using his boat building skills. In that year he decided to come west with his wife to Benton Harbor, Michigan. After checking out the area for business opportunities, Williams went into the lumber business, owning a sawmill and buying timber land. One of his purchases in 1880 was for 540 acres of timber land which included over half a mile of Paw Paw Lake frontage. He paid $16,400 or just over $300 an acre for this tract of land. By this time Williams had a boat, the Skylark, to carry his freight to market in Chicago. Competition quickly sprang up between himself and J.H. Graham, who also owned a saw mill, timber lands, and a boat called the Messenger. The two men decided to consolidate their business interests and with a third partner started the Graham and Morton Transportation Co. Williams subsequently broke that business relationship, moved to South Haven, Michigan in 1888 and started a rival ship company. All through the 1890's Williams four ships: The H. W. Williams 1888, The Glen 1890, The Lorain L. 1891, and the City of Kalamazoo 1893, carried freight and passengers to and from Chicago.

By the latter part of the 1890's, Williams interest also turned to his Paw Paw Lake property. He had part of his land surveyed for a rail line by the South Haven and Eastern Railroad Company from South Haven to the north shore of Paw Paw Lake. In 1899, he built a two story house bordering the lake for himself and his family. In June of 1900, he added a new hotel to his lake property to be known as the Forest Home. During this period, the section of Paw Paw Lake bordering his land started to be called Williams Bay. While on a trip to Baltimore in 1901, Williams died of pneumonia at the age of 72. His son, Charles W. Williams, took over running what had become a large resort complex with a hotel for vacationers and a huge park for campers and day picnickers. In 1908 C. W. Williams sold all of the property to Alfred Nordeen of Chicago thus ending, one of Southwestern Michigan's more successful business pioneer's connection to Paw Paw Lake.

THE JEWELER

Leopold P. Husen was born in Danzig, Germany, in 1852. It was the custom for young men to learn a trade and by the time Husen was a teenager, he was an apprenticed watchmaker. At 18 he immigrated to America to follow his dream of owning his own business and over the next few years he worked diligently and saved his money. His dreams became a reality in 1875 when he opened his first jewelry store in Hartford, Michigan, and soon married Luella Raven, a local girl.

By the late 1880's he was a well known successful businessman who had even opened another jewelry store in Coloma, Michigan. Having seen the refreshing waters of Paw Paw Lake, he decided to build a cottage on it for his family. In 1887, he erected a cottage called the Alpha at Smith's Landing. Being an astute businessman Husen saw the possibilities of the lake becoming a popular resort destination. After his success with Forest Beach, Husen proceeded to buy 17 more acres of land on the Watervliet side of the lake. He broke this property into lots and called the resort subdivision Beachwood Point. The Watervliet Record newspaper of 1895 reported that Husen had received an inheritance and was closing his jewelry shops in Hartford and Coloma. He planned to devote his full time to the development of his lake properties.

Over the next 15 years, through his hard work and effort, Husen helped make the golden era of Paw Paw Lake a reality. He made Beechwood Point the most desirable and fashionable place to buy and have a cottage. Husen erected the Beechwood Pavilion and operated it for 10 years when he sold it to Michael Zimay in 1908. He also had a partnership with Woodward's Pavilion during this period. Husen retired to a splendid home on Beechwood Point to enjoy the rewards of his labor. He continued to be an active man in the community and was still fixing watches in 1936 when he died at the age of 84.

THE INVENTOR

Morris Wood was born in Sacketts Harbor, New York, in 1837. He came to Illinois in 1856, and opened a business as a gunsmith in Hennipen. After the Chicago fire of 1871, Wood left Hennipen and came to Chicago where he started a wood working business. His interests and talents were multi-faceted. He patented a number of drills used in building anything made of wood. He invented a type of drill which was used in making the Panama Canal. Wood also became involved in making some early automobiles.

His first visit to Paw Paw Lake was in 1893. Wood was so favorably impressed with the lake that he leased several cottages and built three more with the intention of making his land part of the booming resort business. He hired a company to sound the lake and was the first person to have a map made of all the depths. Wood became part owner and developer of the first telephone service, which was called the Watervliet and Paw Paw Lake Telephone Co. He also bought 12 acres on the Paw Paw River near Bowe's Landing with the desire to build cottages. After he developed that area into a resort complex, Wood planned to buy and run a river steamer to and from Watervliet. Back at his factory in Chicago, Wood had flyers printed exalting the virtues of Paw Paw Lake as a vacationer's paradise. He included a flyer in each one of his 50,000 tool catalogues going out each year. It was his death in 1905 at age 68 which finally ended his active involvement in the lake. His family continued a link with Paw Paw Lake for two more generations and still carry on the business of Morris Wood Tool Co. in Morristown, Tennessee.

THE REALTOR

George E. Klotter was born in Chicago, Illionis, in 1885. His father, David came to Paw Paw Lake around 1900 to vacation and invest in property. Klotter grew up coming out each summer to enjoy the lake. By the time he reached adulthood, Klotter was involved in a number of ventures. He owned a bar in Chicago, ran the restaurant portion of Woodward's Pavilion, and in 1911 bought the Tumblingrun Hotel and surrounding 40 acres. During the 1920's between real estate deals and playing the stock market, Klotter became a wealthy man. By his 40th birthday he was able to retire to Paw Paw Lake where he built a large home on Alma Island with a spectacular view of the lake. However, with his energy and interests, he could not stay retired for very long.

By 1927, George E. Klotter had amassed over 700 acres of land, islands, and marshlands at the southwestern end of Paw Paw Lake. He planned, as one newspaper called it, "The Venice of the North." Klotter wanted the whole area made into a series of islands connected to each other and the mainland by bridges. The 500 building sites would be connected by channels to the lake. A project of this size and magnitude had never been undertaken in this part of Michigan. In fact, three contractors turned down the job as being too difficult. Finally the firm of Milburn, Gresse, and Cox of Charlotte, Michigan, took the project and in the fall of 1928 started on the Wil-O-Paw Islands. The complexity and scope of this undertaking was so great that articles were written about it in the trade journals of the time. This venture by Klotter and his son was planned to take five years to complete and cost over $750,000. The combination of mother nature, engineering problems and the 1929 stock market crash, took its toll on Klotter's dream for a "City of Islands." During the 1930's, Klotter sold lots on the developed sections of the islands, when he could find buyers but no new dredging or new work was started. With his islands project on hold Klotter decided to build and run a bar and restaurant which he called the Wil-O-Paw. He kept this business until 1944 when he sold it. In 1947 Klotter sold the whole Wil-O-Paw Islands complex to Coats and Cairns, two real estate developers who planned to continue development of the islands where Klotter had stopped and finish developing the "Paw Paw Islands." He retired once more and moved to California where in 1967 George E. Klotter, the biggest and grandest developer of Paw Paw Lake, passed away.

Chapter 6

<u>ELLINEE</u>

It began as "Ernie's Peanut Stand." This was the nickname Ernest H. Erickson's sister good naturally gave to her brother's business venture in the rural wilds of Michigan. From that humble beginning grew an institution that was not only a landmark but also synonymous with Paw Paw Lake itself.

Ernie, as he liked to be called, first came to this area as a boy to attend church camp. By the time he was a young man, his connection to Paw Paw Lake was still strong, and he decided to start a summer business. In 1906 he bought corner lots of the Summer Home subdivision from the estate of George Strong.

What started out as a small store over the years became a complex of buildings spread over many acres of land. During the Ellinee's peak years, with the help of his wife, Hildegard, daughters Dorothy and Frene, Ernie had a workforce of some 35 people running and maintaining the Paw Paw Lake's "Social Center."

A Busy Corner at Lake Point, Paw Paw Lake, Mich.

From a 1912 photograph of the Ellinee (Notice the Interurban)

After buying the property in 1906, Erickson built his first building with his father's help and expertise as a building contractor. By 1908 Erickson opened a souvenir and refreshment store at the corner to Lakewood Point, one block from Baker's Bay on Paw Paw Lake. By 1913 Erickson enlarged his building so he could have box ball alleys (a miniature version of bowling), and in 1914 he put in a new soda fountain. After every summer season Erickson spent his winters thinking about new creative additions to the Ellinee. Each season there always seemed to be a work crew at the Ellinee enlarging, expanding or improving something.

Ellinee Pavilion and Art Club, Paw Paw Lake, Coloma, Mich.   52505-nr

A late 1920's view of the whole Ellinee complex.

Throughout the 1920's Erickson added new activities and buildings. One project would lead into other projects. An example of this was when he put in a 3 lane bowling alley. Erickson built an annex to house the bowling alley where he also put billiard tables and box bowling alleys. The vacant space that was left was then turned into a dance floor with music furnished by an electric piano. By the mid 1920's Erickson had acquired the property down to the lake with frontage on Baker's Bay. He immediately started changing and improving that property. Erickson built a 100 foot long pier to accommodate boaters and bathers and he planned to erect bath houses. He had a large work crew come and remove a hill which blocked some of the view from the Ellinee.

One of Ernie's drivers getting ready for a run into Coloma and Benton Harbor.

By the spring of 1920 the inter-urban line to Paw Paw Lake was out of business. The automobile took its place. However, much of the public, especially from the city, still did not own cars. Erickson, always trying to provide for his customers, decided to start a bus service to take the place of trains. He bought two buses and ran them on a regular schedule to and from the lake. His buses would meet people at the boat dock in Benton Harbor or the train station in Coloma, and transport them and their luggage to Paw Paw Lake. Erickson provided this service through 1924 when he then sold the business. Even though Erickson sold the buses, he made sure in the contract that any future bus lines would always stop at the Ellinee.

NEW SUMMER SCHOOL WILL MEAN
MUCH TO LOCAL RESORT INTERESTS

A 1923 newspaper illustration of the Art School.

By 1923 Erickson built and started an art school. The summer art colony consisted of a school and clubhouse for students and artists. The headquarters of the colony consisted of two buildings connected by a walled court. One building was the school's studio, containing an exhibition room, supply rooms, and an office. The other building was the club quarters, a large 60 x 36 foot room containing a raised stage and open fireplace, and had adjoining rooms for the storage of the members' equipment and canvases.

The school was open from June 1 to September 1 for students and their instructors. In 1928 an arts and crafts department was added to the school. The school attracted artists and students from all over the area. Its summer exhibitions became highlights of the social scene.

ELLINEE VILLAGE INN
<<   >>   BILL OF FARE   <<   >>

```
┌──────────────┐
│   DINNERS    │
└──────────────┘
```

CHICKEN, STEAK OR FISH DINNERS   -   -   - $1.00
FROG LEGS DINNERS   -   -   - $1.25

* * *   CONSISTING OF   * * *

SHRIMP COCKTAIL   FRUIT BOWL   SALAD
CONSOMME   SOUP
CHOICE OF VEGETABLES and FRENCH FRIES
DESSERT   BEER OR COFFEE

```
┌────────────────────────────────────────────────────┐
│    A 1932 Menu From the Ellinee Village Inn.        │
└────────────────────────────────────────────────────┘
```

With the depression came the end of the art school. Jobs were too scarce for instructors to take off for the summer and teach students. In 1932 Ernie converted the buildings into the Ellinee Village Inn. In the largest room he built a facsimile of a village and cottages along the walls. This village surrounded the dining and dance floor area. The cottages were complete with awnings, fences and the roofs were thatched, shingled, or tiled. One of the buildings represented a village theater, another the delicatessen and meat market, and the stage at one end of the large room was transformed into a circus. Liquor was legal again and Ernie would bring entertainers from Chicago to put on two nightly floor shows on weekends. Folks could come and have a full course dinner, dance, and see a floor show all right there at Paw Paw Lake.

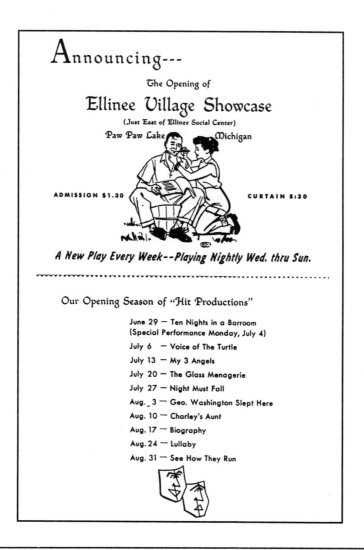

Announcing---

The Opening of

Ellinee Village Showcase

(Just East of Ellinee Social Center)

Paw Paw Lake   Michigan

ADMISSION $1.30   CURTAIN 8:30

A New Play Every Week--Playing Nightly Wed. thru Sun.

Our Opening Season of "Hit Productions"

June 29 — Ten Nights in a Barroom
(Special Performance Monday, July 4)

July 6 — Voice of The Turtle

July 13 — My 3 Angels

July 20 — The Glass Menagerie

July 27 — Night Must Fall

Aug. 3 — Geo. Washington Slept Here

Aug. 10 — Charley's Aunt

Aug. 17 — Biography

Aug. 24 — Lullaby

Aug. 31 — See How They Run

A Program showing the plays for the season.

By 1938 Erickson closed the nightclub and moved the bar and restaurant over to the main building. For a period in 1944 the building was rented to Harry Liberman for his lawn and children's furniture business. After that business left, the old Art School buildings stood empty. In 1955, Erickson leased the main building for a summer playhouse. For the next eight years the summer theater brought people to this part of the Ellinee complex.

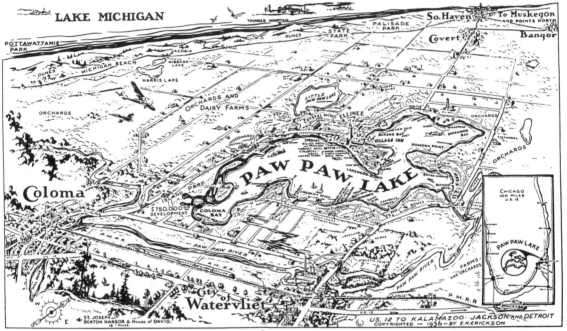

SOUTHERN MICHIGAN'S LARGEST INLAND LAKE

This map was first drawn by Ernest H. Erickson in 1930 for a resort pamphlet. He updated and changed it in 1936, 1948, and 1955)

Erickson stayed active and ran the Ellinee up to his death in 1969. His daughter Ferne closed the Ellinee in 1971 and was forced to tear it down because of its age and insurance liability. Even though Erickson and the Ellinee are gone, his memory and talent continue on through his art work. Ernest H. Erickson's map of Paw Paw Lakes and the surrounding area continues to carry on his legacy.

Chapter 7

CRYSTAL PALACE

The comment "how did I every get into this" by Frank Dlouhy is probably the best way to start the story of the Crystal Palace. Those first couple of years he said that comment to himself many times as he went about making this ballroom a success.

He was a second generation immigrant who, by his training and hard work, had become a successful Chicago carpenter and building contractor. By the 1920's, Dlouhy was living the "American Dream" and happily building houses in Chicago. In 1924 Richard Macek, his brother-in-law, approached him with a plan to build a dance hall. Macek had purchased property on a popular resort lake in Michigan and needed help building a pavilion. Dlouhy said yes based on the pure challenge of the project. Starting with no blueprints or work force, Dlouhy proceeded to plan, organize and build the Crystal Palace Ballroom at Paw Paw Lake.

CRYSTAL PALACE

Throughout the spring of 1925, people from the area watched and waited for the opening of, as the local papers said, "The finest dancing casino in the state of Michigan." There was even a local contest to name the new dance pavilion. The name Crystal Palace captured first place with Dreamland earning a second and Wolverine a third. The price was divided equally between Gerald Coon of Watervliet and Miss Celia Umphrey of Coloma. Everything was ready for the opening dedication on Saturday evening, April 25, 1925.

On April 19 a mysterious fire destroyed the new building. The only thing salvaged was a new grand concert piano from the fire. Gasoline cans were found next to the smoldering remains, and a $1,000 reward was offered for any information about the people responsible for this "villainous" act. No one was ever arrested for the fire. All the next day cars drove by filled with people who came to see the destruction. To their surprise, they were met by a sign put up by Dlouhy and Macek proclaiming that a bigger and finer Crystal Palace would be rebuilt as soon as possible. Frank Dlouhy had decided to provide his own money and time into rebuilding the pavilion thus making a commitment to Paw Paw Lake for the rest of his life.

The rebuilding of the Crystal Palace exemplifies Paw Paw Lake at its finest. The outpouring of community spirit and support to help was phenomenal. The local newspapers kept a running commentary of the rebuilding. The Watervliet-Coloma American Legion Post came as a group one weekend to help finish putting on the roof. By May 30, 1925, only five weeks after the fire had burnt it to the ground, a new Crystal Palace Ballroom was open for business.

A 1925 postcard shot of the Crystal Palace.

The photograph above shows how the Crystal Palace looked when it first opened in 1925. At that time the Pavilion was not covered with siding and stood as this beautiful white wooden structure. This picture is taken from the end of a wooden pier which provided access from the lake to the Crystal Palace. The concrete breakwater pier, and lights were added at a later time.

73

Two outside views of the Crystal Palace.

1927 view of the inside. (Notice the stage in the middle on the left hand side. This is where the band would play because it was before an amplified sound system was available)

Another view of the dance floor. (Notice the flyers on the posters advertising Lawrence Welk and his band coming to the Crystal Palace.

Crystal Palace

Paw Paw Lake, Coloma, Mich.

DANCING

TO

Chas. Armstead's Orchestra

MISSOURI'S MOST POPULAR BAND

FEATURE NITES!

Monday   **Request Nite**

Come and have the boys play your favorite tunes.

Tuesday   **Fox Trot Contest**

Two Beautiful Loving Cups to the winners.

Wednesday   **Appreciation Nite**

Free admission.   Five cents a dance.

Thursday   **Amateur Nite**

Prizes to the winners.

Friday   **Waltz Contest**

Two Beautiful Loving Cups to the Winners.

Poster from the 1930's for the house band which played every night during summer.

A late 1920's photo of the Crystal Palace Baseball Team.

One of Dlouhy's passions was baseball. If he had a chance to pursue any other career it would have been as a baseball player. Having his own team was the next best alternative. The Crystal Palace "Blues" were formed as a baseball team and became part of the local baseball circuit. Dlouhy built a baseball field, dugout and bleachers behind the Crystal Palace. Every Sunday afternoon in the summer time you heard the crack of a bat and the roar of a crowd as the "Blues" took to the mound. This team was good enough that in the fall a number of times they played the famous House of David team of Benton Harbor, Michigan for the Southwestern Michigan Championship.

CRYSTAL PALACE

Paw Paw Lake, Coloma, Mich.

presents

Louis 'Satchmo' Armstrong

and His All Stars

Saturday, June 16th

Adm. $2.00 per person — Tax Inc.

CRYSTAL PALACE

Paw Paw Lake, Coloma, Mich.

presents

THE INCOMPARABLE

Wayne King

HIS GOLDEN SAXOPHONE

— and his —

WORLD FAMOUS ORCHESTRA

Saturday, June 8th

Adm. $1.75 per person — Tax Included

DANCING EVERY SATURDAY NITE

These band advertisements were postcards sent out weekly by mail to 1500 people telling them who was coming to the Crystal Palace next.

The 1930's and 1940's were known as the big band era in America. One of the primary means of entertainment for this nation was listening or dancing to the music of these bands. Many of these bands made a regular circuit of stops across the United States. Because of its size and booking only union bands the Crystal Palace was able to attract all of the great bands. Jimmy and Tommy Dorsey, Les Brown, Duke Ellington, Woody Herman and Count Basie are just some of the bands that played the Crystal Palace Ballroom.

Merv Griffin

Perry Como

Doris Day

Three of the vocalists who sang at the Crystal Palace

CRYSTAL PALACE   Chapter 7

The Crystal Palace was a ballroom to thousands of people but provided much more than just music or dancing to the local communities. Frank Dlouhy believed in giving back to his community. Through the years the Crystal Palace was host to about every kind of function imaginable. Every Sunday in the summer time it was used by the St. Joseph Catholic Church of Watervliet to hold mass because the numbers were so great the local church could not accommodate them all. Countless businesses and factories held their annual picnics on the grounds of the Crystal Palace. Events from wedding receptions to town hall meetings were held under the Crystal Palace's roof. The New Year's Eve party held each year was legendary.

For 37 years two generations of the Dlouhy family ran this Paw Paw Lake landmark. Dlouhy's wife, Bessie, sold tickets and their three children Ray, Elinor, and Vi managed the other tasks of running a ballroom. Ray became a partner with his father in 1946 and his wife Dorothy and son Brad continued the same family tradition. The Crystal Palace Ballroom was sold in 1962 and was being converted to a roller rink when it was destroyed by fire in February of 1963.

Chapter 8

PAVILIONS

The Crystal Palace might have been the most famous dance pavilion but was preceded by other pavilions around the lake. During the first part of the century these pavilions provided the major source of activities for vacationers. Many of the younger people, by land and water, would make a circuit of going to all of them on a Saturday night.

Woodwards Pavilion on the Coloma side of the lake was the biggest and oldest having been erected in 1899. It set the standard for recreation at Paw Paw Lake. The huge dance floor, billiard tables, bowling alley, and refreshment parlor provided activities for everyone. Part of this structure was built over the water and planned so people could promenade back and forth. During the summertime various bands would provide music nightly with some theme and favors included for the participants. In the afternoons dancing lessons would be offered free of charge to anyone interested with blinds pulled down to provide privacy. All the other pavilions on the lake supplied their own version of these activities and each tried to outdo the other for the resorter's business.

THE WOODWARD PAVILION

A. H. Woodward
Proprietor

Prof. S. P. DALBROOK of Chicago, *Master of Ceremonies*

Select Dancing Parties given every evening during the week, except Sunday.
Bowling every evening.   Boats and Launches for hire.
Billiard and Pool Tables.   Refreshments of all kinds.

Opening Party, Saturday Evening, June 29, 1907

Music by the popular and well known Lawrence Orchestra.   Chas. A. Lawrence, Musical Director.

From a 1907 resort guide about Paw Paw Lake

Early photograph of Woodward's Pavilion.

Two interior views of Woodward's Pavilion.

Two views of the Beechwood Pavilion.

Forest Beach Pavilion

UNDER NEW MANAGEMENT

Frank Ollinger, Proprietor   H. E. Moore, Manager

ROLLER RINK

Our $1,500 Military Band Organ furnishes music at all sessions

For Amusements

Brunswick-Balke Regulation Pool and Billiard Tables

High Class Roller Rink   300 Winslow Skates   Three New Bowling Alleys

A large line of Souvenir Postal Cards, Fine Cigars and Tobaccos, Candies, Ice Cream Sodas.

K-7 on map   LUNCH COUNTER

From a 1907 brochure about Paw Paw Lake.

EDGEWATER BEACH.   WATERVLIET, MICH.

View of Forest Beach Pavilion and Edgewater Pavilion.

"THE CASTLE ON THE HILL"

FOREST GLEN PAVILION

Beechwood Point, Paw Paw Lake

WATERVLIET, MICHIGAN

Now in the Course of Construction

WILL BE COMPLETED, FURNISHED AND READY FOR BUSINESS BY JUNE 1st, 1911

The Largest Dance Hall In Southern Michigan

The most completely equipped amusement Pavilion on the Lake. Bowling Alleys, Billiard and Pool Rooms. Refreshment Adjunct par excellence. The purest Ice Cream, Soda Water and Soft Drinks of every description. Candy, Fruit and Cigar Stands in Corridor. A fully appointed Short Order Restaurant and Lunch Room. Souvenirs, Indian Curios, etc., etc. Convenient, commodious Waiting and Toilet Rooms. Garage and Stables for Autos and Horses. Special attention given to Automobile Parties.

In fact FOREST GLEN PAVILION will contain every comfort and

convenience required by Summer Resorters and Tourists.

Forest Glen Pavilion is situated on the most delightful spot on the most beautiful inland Lake in Michigan. From the elegant wide verandas can be viewed the Lake in its entirety and also a landscape view is afforded which passes description. From the high elevation of the Pavilion can be enjoyed the purest air of every breeze that blows. Here if anywhere on this terrestrial sphere can be enjoyed a real "Breath from Heaven."

Newspaper advertisement in 1911 for Forest Glen Pavilion. This building later became the Cottager's Country Club.

Chapter 9

STORIES

History becomes alive and meaningful to us when we can make a connection with it. The stories in this chapter try to provide some of that meaning. The events that shaped these stories are a cross section of the people, places, and things of Paw Paw Lake. Each story tries to give a different perspective of the life and times of this lake over a century of time. They are laid out in no particular order or importance. Hopefully any significance they have will be in the feelings they evoke for the reader.

The Boneless Camp

One of the more colorful characters that Paw Paw Lake produced was a man by the name of A.R. Linder. He was half American Indian and half Swede. He was also known as the "Liver King." From the middle teens through the 1920's Linder ran a place on Lakewood Point called the Boneless Camp. This establishment was a convenience store and restaurant all under one roof. If you needed some kerosene for your lantern, flour to bake, or nails to build, Lindy (another nickname he went by) had it at his store. His most important business was the restaurant business. Dinner would be served in a room 15 feet by 15 feet with a canoe hanging from the ceiling and one wall having stained glass windows in it. Lindy's specialty was chicken livers - hence the name "Boneless Camp." The following is the sequence your meal would take: A patron would walk in the front door, sit down at a table, and order chicken or chicken livers. Lindy would then go out the back door, catch the chicken, kill it, pluck its feathers, cook it, and serve you minutes later.

Anti-Semitism

Like most places and times in history, Paw Paw Lake wasn't without a few negative aspects of its own. The people who vacationed there or lived there reflected some of the prevailing attitudes of those times.

In the summer of 1908 a family came to vacation at Paw Paw Lake from Chicago. They heard about this delightful resort area with its many hotels and beaches. The parents and two young daughters arrived at a hotel on a weekend when the weather was wet and cold. After checking in at the desk they went to the dining room for dinner. When the family returned to pick up their room keys they were told there had been a mistake and in fact there were no rooms available for them. At this point, with rain and lighting outside, the father told the manager his family could not or would not leave in this weather. A room was somehow found for the night, but the next morning they left to find friendlier lodging. The family later became aware that the attempt to deny them a room was because they were Jewish.

During the first part of the century, this bias against Jewish people was common not only at Paw Paw Lake, but across the country. Some hotels at the lake blatantly advertised no "Jews allowed." There were even legal abstracts from that period describing property and cottages specifying that no Jews were allowed to rent or buy. This anti-semitism was never universally practiced around the lake and with time faded into the past.

The House of Painted Ladies

One summer Sunday morning in the 1920's, a young boy of ten came home from playing. He had some questions to ask his mother because he saw some things he did not understand. He wanted to know about the pretty ladies in the house down the street. This particular morning all of the "ladies" were sitting out on the porch having coffee, laughing, and smoking their cigarettes. Only as an inquisitive ten year old can know, there was something different between these "ladies" and his mother. He wanted to know why they wore makeup and had lipstick on in the morning. His mother never put makeup on before breakfast. The young boy was also curious about the "ladies'" fancy and frilly robes and nightgowns. His mom sure didn't have any like these.

The specific answers given to that young boy by his mother have been lost to time. Only years later, by now a young man, did he discover the truth. There had been a "House of Pleasure" in his neighborhood. Here was a tourist attraction for vacationers that was never in the Paw Paw Lake Resort Guides. Summer guests of the lake could come by water or land to spend a few hours with some bathtub gin and a little companionship. Local lore said there were a couple of these "houses" available for vacationers around the lake during the summertime.

Rivalry

As long as civilization has big cities and small towns, there will always be a rivalry between the two. Each looks down on the other because of their perceived values and morals. Chicago people (residences) versus Coloma and Watervliet people (residence) do not escape this very human condition. The following are two examples of this phenomena.

One Saturday night in the early 1930's a young farmer from the Coloma area went to the Crystal Place to dance. While there, he met a young woman vacationing with her girlfriend from Chicago. After a courtship, they married and settled down in this area. Having been married for some time the couple sat down to have an honest husband and wife discussion. He reported to her that some of their neighbors and town folks thought that she was "snotty" and "stand-offish" because she did not acknowledge or say hello to people when she was in town or shopping. She responded that her big city upbringing taught her it was not polite or proper to respond to strangers. It wasn't until they had this conversation that they both were able to see each other's point of view, and understand their different backgrounds brought about different responses.

Another example of this animosity between the two can be seen in a poem sent into the Coloma Courier in 1899.

THE SUMMER PAW PAW LAKER   by: H.B.B.

Under a spreading Beechwood tree
The girl from the city stands;
A naughty saucy air has she,
With big and bony hands,
And muscles on her bicycle foot
Are strong as leather bands.

Her hair is frizzled and frowzled and long
She's covered with freckles and tan,
Her brow is wet with salty sweat
For she travels where ever she can
And stares the Jays and Reubs in the face,
For she is not afraid of a man.

Day in, day out, from dawn till dark
You can hear her whoop and blow,
While she swings the oaken oar around
With a measured beat and slow,
Like a drayman whipping a fractious mule
When he wants to make him go.

She goes on Sundays to the church,
She sits and stares at boys
And slyly grins when the parson prays
But she doesn't make any noise.
When she hears false notes from the choir bass
It makes her heart rejoice.

Through forest and field the country wide
Tearing, ripping around she goes.
Each morning sees her, needle in hand,
Mending the rents in her clothes.
By the time night rolls around again
She's tried enough for repose.

The home girls walking along the road,
Peep in at her cottage door
And say to each other, "how we wish
She wouldn't come here any more
To take our country manners off
And be a perfect bore."

To her it sounds like an echo from
The bull frog in the brake,
The semblance causing her to laugh
With a deep convulsive shake, and
With a kerchief hiding her swimming eyes,
Which she wipes for politeness sake.

Cranks, cranks! These city girls must be
If they treat you not as they ought;
For unto our little watering place
The city styles they brought,
And left upon the sandy shore,
Footprints like Crusoe sought.

The Rich Arsonist

One of the standing jokes and recurring rumors of the lake was that somewhere there was a rich, retired arsonist who had specialized in Paw Paw Lake fires. It seemed to be that many establishments either on the verge or having gone out of business would mysteriously burn down. In reality, a number of factors combined to totally destroy any buildings which caught fire. Most of the buildings around the lake were built of southern pine which after it dried out and aged was very combustible. Because of the distance and time to burn, the volunteer fire departments had little left to save. In most incidences the cause was never determined. It was usually reported that the fire had been started by lightning or an electrical problem. This lack of evidence just encouraged the stories through the years.

Drownings

This might seem like an odd subject to write about, but drownings are a part of the life and history of Paw Paw Lake. "First Drowning of the Season" and Paw Paw Lake Takes Another Life," are some of the headlines which would appear each summer in the local newspapers. They were not trying to be sensational or morbid but rather had a matter of fact attitude. Because of the sheer number of people who descended on the lake every summer, it was common for a drowning to occur. The victims were usually young people who accidentally were taken by the waters of Paw Paw Lake. Some summers there were a number of drownings, and it would produce a gloom over the whole lake. The lake has no safe season because many a winter there was also a drowning on Paw Paw Lake. Luckily, in recent times, those tragedies have diminished so that a drowning is the exception rather than the rule.

The Hamburger King

One of the more famous people associated with Paw Paw Lake was Ray Kroc, founder of McDonalds. In the summer of 1919, Kroc, as a young man, came to Paw Paw Lake to play piano in a band at the Edgewater Pavilion. In his autobiography with Robert Anderson, Grinding it Out, he talks about how wonderful those experiences were at the lake and how he was one of the "Charleston-crazed kids." He explains how the band would board one of the boats and play various tunes while cruising along the shore line. One of the band members would periodically stand up in the bow calling out with a megaphone "Dancing tonight at the Edgewater, don't miss out on the fun!" Kroc met his first wife, Ethel Fleming, during that summer at Paw Paw Lake. She was one of the daughters of the owners of the May-Bell Hotel at Lakewood Point.

A few years went by and Kroc, by now, was working for a paper company in Chicago selling and supplying paper goods. Part of his territory was the Paw Paw Lake area and one of his accounts was the Ellinee. The combination of his past connections with Paw Paw Lake and his business account made him a regular customer at the Ellinee and a friend of Ernie Erickson. Years later Kroc came back to Ernie Erickson with his idea about a hamburger chain. Through their years of friendship and business dealings he knew Ernie was a man of vision and always interested in a new challenge. Kroc wanted to help set up Erickson in one of his new hamburger franchises but Ernie said he was too old to start a new venture and wished him good luck.

The Paw Paw Lake Alligator

In the summer of 1919, A.R. Linder, owner of the Boneless Camp, returned to Paw Paw Lake with an alligator from Florida. He placed it in a tank in the front of his restaurant. It provided, as he had hoped, to be quite the tourist attraction. At some point Linder decided the tank was cramping the alligator and took it down to the lake for some exercise. He attached a rope to the alligator so it couldn't get loose. Well, at some point the rope broke and off swam the reptile into the depths of Paw Paw Lake, never to be confined again. Through the years there were numerous unconfirmed sightings of this creature and the story was told by many mothers who wanted their children out of the water.

For any doubters of this story let this 1929 Coloma Courier article lay their skepticism to rest.

"LIVE ALLIGATOR WAS CAUGHT IN CREEK NORTH OF COLOMA"

A real, live alligator measuring over three feet in length was captured in Rogers Creek, north of Coloma, a few weeks ago by Floyd Dunbar, who was hunting along the banks of the stream and was attracted by bulging eyes of the reptile, which made a dive for him, then scampered into the water. Floyd secured a fish net and captured the alligator, which he sold to John A. Rorick, who has had it on exhibition at his feed mill this week, but has sold the pet and it will be shipped to LaPorte, Indiana. It is believed that the alligator was brought from the south by some of those wintering there and made its escape to the creek. It is thought that the reptile is about twelve years old.

Ice Harvest

Most of the history and activities around Paw Paw Lake are associated with summertime. What most people are not aware of is that in wintertime the lake also provided jobs and produced a cash crop. That crop was blocks of ice to be used for refrigeration purposes by hotels, restaurant and individuals. From before the turn of the century through the 1930's tons of ice were taken each winter from the lake. This process was known as the ice harvest. Through the years a number of huge ice houses had been erected at the lake's edge. Every winter after the lake froze, over 150 men took part in harvesting the ice. A channel from the ice house was cut out into the lake and blocks would then be cut off. Two men on both sides of the channel with long poles would guide the block of ice to shore. The block would then be put on a conveyor belt that ran up into the ice house. Men inside would stack the blocks of ice with sawdust between them. Here, the blocks of ice would sit until they were shipped out or individuals would pick them up to use in their home or cottage.

Chapter 10

THEN AND NOW

This front cover is from a 1909 postcard packet which contained 12 pictures of Paw Paw Lake and the area.

Over the years many pictures were taken of the lake and sent as postcards. This chapter takes a few of those scenes and compares them to their 1994 location.

GETTING READY FOR THE MOTOR BOAT RACES AT CRYSTAL PALACE
Paw Paw Lake, Coloma, Michigan   87759

From a 1940's postcard.

Current picture of same location dated 1993.

From a 1917 postcard.

Current picture of same location dated 1993.

Douglas View, Paw Paw Lake, Mich.

Current picture of same location dated 1993.

From a 1915 postcard.

Current picture of same location dated 1993.

The Terminal Lake Point, Paw Paw Lake, Mich.

From a 1910 postcard.

Current picture of same location dated 1993.

THE WIGWAM HOTEL - PAW PAW LAKE, COLOMA, MICHIGAN   52550 NR

From a 1944 postcard.

Current picture of same location dated 1993.

LAKE POINT, PAW PAW LAKE, MICH.

From a 1912 postcard.

Current picture of same location dated 1993.

Chapter 11

FACTS ABOUT THE LAKE

The following list of facts, in alphabetical order, provide some of the information about Paw Paw Lake. Many will be informative and others just whimsical.

*A*lma - The name of the main island and largest one in what has been known as the Paw Paw Lake Islands or Wil-O-Paw Islands.

*B*ays - Historically there have been four bays at Paw Paw Lake. Each bay's name was associated with a person who owned lake frontage on that bay or had some impact on it. Through the years some of these changed names as the people who influenced them changed.

1. Williams Bay was named for the ship owner H. W. Williams from South Haven, Michigan. This bay then became known as Baker's Bay for the physician Dr. W. A. Baker of Coloma. This Bay is now known as the Ellinee Bay based on when it was a part of the Ellinee complex.

2. Sherwood Bay is the only one which has kept the same name through the years. It was named for Harvey C. Sherwood a very prominent Watervliet farmer whose land bordered part of this Bay.

3. Outlet Bay was so named because this is where a tributary flows out of Paw Paw Lake to the Paw Paw River. This Bay is more typically known as Smitty's or Bowe's Landing.

4. Curtis Bay was named for a farmer whose farm fronted the Bay. It then was called Coloma Bay for a number of years. The Bay is now known as Douglas Bay for a dentist, Dr. P. E. Douglas who operated and owned a resort complex called Douglas View Resort.

*C*ensus - The 1990 United States Government population count for Paw Paw Lake is a total of 3782 people. Broken down, there are 2588 on the Coloma side and 1194 on the Watervliet side. These numbers include people not directly on the lake.

*D*epth - The mean depth of the lake is estimated at 35 feet with the deepest point being over 90 feet deep.

*E*lectricity - In May of 1913 for the first time people around Paw Paw Lake were able to make application for electricity to be brought to their homes.

*F*amilies - Many of the businesses around Paw Paw Lake were owned and operated as a family enterprise with each member having their responsibilities and tasks. This definition of families is to honor and recognize their importance and work to the success of Paw Paw Lake.

*G*arfish - The name given to a predatory fish belonging to the genus lepisosteus. They are easily identified by their long slender silvery body with jaw and teeth that form a ferocious looking mouth. They were hunted on a regular basis in Paw Paw Lake with the intent to exterminate them.

*H*oneydipper - Man The nickname of the man who came to your cottage initially by wagon and then truck carrying big barrels. His task was to clean out the waste from your outhouse by bucket and carry it away in those big barrels.

*I*ndians - The Pottawattamie Tribes, whose name means, "People of the Place of Fire;" were the last group of Indians to live in the Paw Paw Lake area.

*J*amirilo - The name one family gave to their boat. It is derived from the first two letters of each member of that family. It has been and continues to be customary to give a name to the boat you own.

*K*erosene - Until electricity came to Paw Paw Lake this fuel oil was the primary source of energy. It was used for lighting, heating and cooking.

*L*atitude & *L*ongitude - Paw Paw Lake is 42 degrees 12 minutes and 8 seconds north latitude and is 86 degrees 16 minutes and 4 seconds west longitude.

*M*iles - Based on the U.S. Corp. of Engineers statistics, the shore line around Paw Paw Lake is 9.2 miles. If the 3 islands are included the total mileage is almost 11 miles.

*N*aphtha - A liquid made from petroleum or coal tar used as a fuel. Many of the early boats on the lake used this fuel as their source of power.

*O*utlet - The name of the natural tributary which in normal conditions flows out of Paw Paw Lake and connects with the Paw Paw River.

*P*aw *P*aw - A fleshy fruit from a tree which typically grows on stream banks. It has a taste between a banana and a pear. The scientific name for this fruit is Asimina triloba.

*Q*uiz *K*ids - The name of a popular 1940's radio show and early 1950's television show. The emcee of the show was Joe Kelly who had a cottage on Sherwood Bay.

*R*iparian *R*ights - Any person that owns land that abuts an inland lake or stream is a "Riparian" land owner. In the state of Michigan those owners have exclusive rights to the submerged lands fronting their property with a few exceptions.

*S*prings - The sources of most of the water in Paw Paw Lake. There are a number of spring locations under the lake flowing into the lake.

*T*ownship - From 1846 through 1917 all of Paw Paw Lake and the town of Coloma were part of Watervliet township. In 1917 they were split into separate townships of Coloma and Watervliet.

***U*nderwater *E*xhaust** - By Michigan law all boats with an outboard motor must have their exhaust below the water surface.

***V*olume** - According to the U.S. Corp of Engineers the volume of Paw Paw Lake is 1,260,000,000 cubic feet.

***W*idth** - In one section of Paw Paw Lake the lake is one half mile wide.

***X*anadu** - The word comes from a poem by Samuel T. Coleridge which represents a place of idyllic beauty. This was the name given to one of the cottages at Paw Paw Lake. It is the custom to give your cottage a name.

***Y*acht *C*lub** - In 1906 papers were filed to incorporate the first yacht club on Paw Paw Lake. The first commodore was Dr. P. E. Douglas.

***Z*erelda** - The name of one of the steam boats that started service in 1894 taking passengers around the lake.

Chapter 12

<u>REFLECTIONS</u>

As the author, my dilemma became how to end this book. As long as people continue to enjoy the waters of Paw Paw Lake, there can be no last chapter. Instead I have chosen to use a series of drawings to capture the essence of Paw Paw Lake as a final chapter. Each one of these drawings represents part of the lake's history, happy times for countless numbers of vacationers, and memories for generations of families.

THE BOATHOUSE

This drawing of a boathouse on the opposite page is one of the few boat houses still standing that once lined the lake. During the first part of the century these boathouses were very common, and each one seemed to be bigger than the next. They served a number of functions for the summer cottage owners. On the practical side, the boathouses provided a place to dock and store boats. Often these buildings were two stories and had sleeping quarters for the children or guests upstairs. These boathouses also provided a certain level of status for the owners. The presence of a boathouse indicated that not only could the owner afford a cottage and lake property, but also had the money for boats as well.

THE EGG CRATE

The Egg Crate on the opposite page is representative of the country life city people wanted. These eggs provided a connection between the two life styles. Here was opportunity to bring back a part of Paw Paw Lake. This Egg Crate, or others like it, would take the following journey. On Sunday night before going back to Chicago, a family would take this crate to one of the farmers around Paw Paw Lake. Monday morning the farmer would fill the crate with fresh eggs and take them to town. At this point the United States Post Office would stamp the egg crate and send it through the mail service (hard to believe but true). By Wednesday or Thursday morning that family in Chicago would be enjoying Michigan country eggs for breakfast.

The Egg Crate

Sherry Holland

THE WATER PUMP

The drawing on the opposite page is of an old-fashioned water pump. This functioning pump is the only one remaining at Fairview Beach on the Watervliet side of the lake. It sits on its own ten by ten foot deeded and titled piece of property. This particular pump has served the needs of eight cottages for almost a hundred years.

Because property on Pomona Point was initially leased to vacationers, common wells were dug for groups of cottages. Through the years different families would take turns collecting money from the other cottage owners and pay the taxes. This last surviving pump represents a lifestyle of common bonds not only for generations of resorters on Fairview Beach but all vacationers that shared some part of Paw Paw Lake with each other.

HONEYMOON

A book on Paw Paw Lake would not be complete without a statement and picture of the boat called the Honeymoon. The drawing on the opposite page showing the Honeymoon will take us back down memory lane. It seems like everyone that ever came to Paw Paw Lake or lived in this area took a ride on the Honeymoon at one time or another.

The boat was 42 feet long and 10 feet wide. It had two decks and could accommodate up to 65 passengers. The Honeymoon would pick people up from the docks around the lake and transport them up and down the river to Watervliet. This boat represents the last one of a fleet of similar boats that piled the waters of the lake during its heyday as a resort destination. The Honeymoon was the only boat that survived until the 1950's when it too was dry docked forever.

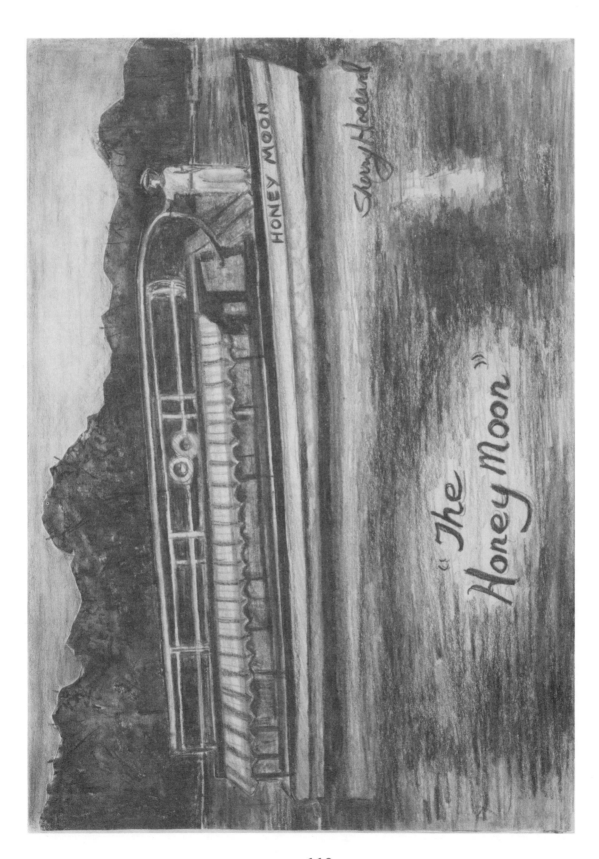

THE UNKNOWN DIVER

What better way to end this first book about Paw Paw Lake than with a mystery. The drawing on the opposite page is taken from an old postcard showing a young man diving into the lake. Who is this young man diving into Paw Paw Lake?

While doing research and interviewing people for this book, I would ask if anyone knew the identity of the diver. I was struck by the intensity and certainty of people's answers. This diver was identified as someone's grandfather, an uncle, a brother, and a father. All were quite sure this diver was their relative. In retrospect, I realized how important this diver or any other symbol of Paw Paw Lake is for people. These symbols represent a connection to all the wonderful feelings and memories toward the lake.

A poem which would appear in many of the resort guides and articles about Paw Paw Lake.

"I don't know how to tell it, but if sech a thing could be
As the angels wantin' boarding and they'd call around on me
I'd want to 'comidate 'em all----the whole enduring flock, And send 'em all
to Paw Paw Lake, if I had to pawn my clock."

(With apologies to James Whitcomb Riley)

AUTHOR'S NOTE

In putting together the materials for this book it quickly became evident I had too much data for one book. Such chapters as Little Paw Paw Lake and Flood Control, the story about Al Capone, the many photographs of the lake, all had to be left out.

Consequently, I am in the process of writing two more books about the lake and surrounding area. The second book to be published will be primarily pictorial and illustrated. The last book to be written will tell the rest of the story and history of the Paw Paw Lake area.

Roderick L. Rasmussen

ACKNOWLEDGEMENTS/SOURCES

This truly became a family project. To my father, Louis W. Rasmussen who through his stories laid the ground work for this book. To my sister, Janie A. Staggers for typing some of the original drafts and her enthusiasm. To my daughter, Katharine P. Rasmussen, for her editing and style suggestions.

One person who made the difference in this book being written is Bill Beverly of Watervliet, Michigan. His sharing of his time, materials, and knowledge about Paw Paw Lake made this book a reality.

The following libraries and historical societies were invaluable for their historical materials and help. The Coloma Public Library staff must be singled out to thank for their support and cooperation.

Benton Harbor Public Library - Benton Harbor, Michigan

Berrien County Historical Society - Berrien Springs, Michigan

Chicago Historical Society, Chicago, Illinois

Coloma Public Library - Coloma, Michigan

Fort Miami Historical Society - St. Joseph, Michigan

Northern Berrien County Historical Society - Coloma, Michigan

South Haven Public Library - South Haven, Michigan

Watervliet Public Library - Watervliet, Michigan

In appreciation to the following people I had interviews with:

Ted Blahnik - Coloma, Michigan

Ferne Erickson Betz - Coloma, Michigan

Bill Beverly - Watervliet, Michigan

Millard Brower - Coloma, Michigan

Helen Livingston Blum - Chicago, Illinois

ACKNOWLEDGEMENTS/SOURCES

(continuation of interviews)

Annabeth Wood Cartwright - Morristown, Tennesse

Ray Dlouhy - Coloma, Michigan

Frank Engel - Grand Rapids, Michigan

Orville Fry - Watervliet, Michigan

Stanley Hansen - Coloma, Michigan

Larry McClanahan - Coloma, Michigan

Genevive and Phyllis Sahlin - St. Joseph, Michigan

Louis Scheid - Watervliet, Michigan

Betty Schwarting Peyton - Deerfield Beach, Flordia

In appreciation to the following people I had conversations with:

Shirley Anderson Cox - Watervliet, Michigan

Bert Deaner - Watervliet, Michigan

Vivian Liberman DuBow - Ft. Wayne, Indiana

Steven Haddad - Paw Paw, Michigan

Bill Hansen - Coloma, Michigan

John Klotter - Orlando, Flordia

Rodney Krieger - Coloma, Michigan

Alice Schrosbree - Watervliet, Michigan

Norman Wilhelmsen - Livonia, Michigan

BIBLIOGRAPHY

Appleyard, Richard, *Images of the Past from the Collection of Richard Appleyard*. Baars Printing Co., Southhaven, Michigan, 1984.

Benet's Reader's Encyclopedia by Harper and Row Publishers, New York, 3rd ed., 1987.

Carney, James T., *Berrien Bicentennial*, Stevensville, Michigan. Tesar Printing Co. 1976.

Chicago Daily News Motor and Resort Guide - Summer 1926. *Chicago Daily News Inc.* Chicago, Illinois, 1926.

Collier's Encyclopedia. P.F. Collier Inc., 866 Third Ave., New York, Copyright 1993.

Coloma Courier Newspaper, November 1889 - 1969, Coloma, Michigan.

Ellis, Franklin, *History of Berrien and Van Buren Counties*, D.W. Ensign, Philadelphia, 1880.

Glimpses of the Past, Published by the Northern Berrien Historical Society. Printed by Tri-City Record, Watervliet, Michigan, 1992.

Kroc Ray, Anderson, Robert, *Grinding it Out:The Making of McDonald's*, Regnery, New York, 1977.

Michigan Riparian Magazine, Feb. 1979, 9620 East Shore Dr., Portage, Michigan, 49081.

Middleton, William D., *The Interurban Era*. Kalmbach Publishing Co., Milwaukee, Wisconsin, Copyright 1961.

Official Guide of Paw Paw Lake 1907-Season. Co-operative Press, Chicago, Illinois 1907.

Stark, Mabel Branch, *Trails From Shingle Diggin's*. R.W. Patterson Printing Co. Benton Harbor, Michigan 1977.

BIBLIOGRAPHY

Tri-City Record Newspaper 1984-1993. Watervliet, Michigan.

U.S. Army Corp of Engineers Detroit District - Paw Paw Lake:Final Detailed Project Report and Environmental Impact Statement. Section 205, Nov. 1983.

United States Department of the Interior Geological Survey. The National Atlas of the United States of America. Washington, D.C. 1970.

Watervliet Record Newspaper 1890-October of 1984 Watervliet, Michigan.

INDEX

INDEX

INDEX

INDEX

INDEX

W

Order Form

To order this book by mail please send your request with

name, address and payment included to:

Southwestern Michigan Publications
P.O. Box 916
Coloma, Michigan 49038
Phone # 616/468-9337

SOFTBOUND		HARDBOUND
$15.85		$27.30
.95	← Michigan sales tax →	1.60
	0 % if shipped out of Michigan	
$16.80		$28.90
2.50	← Shipping & Handling for →	2.50
	1st book and .75 each additional	
$19.30	← TOTAL →	$31.40

Payment: ___ Check or Credit Card ___ Visa/Master Card ___

Card Number _____

Name on Card _____ Exp. Date ____/_____